PENGUIN BOOKS

The New Not-Strictly Vegetarian Cookbook

Lois Dribin and Susan Ivankovich are the authors of two other cookbooks, _The Not-Strictly Vegetarian Cookbook_ and _Cooking with Sun-Dried Tomatoes_. They both live in Bucks County, Pennsylvania, with their husbands and children.

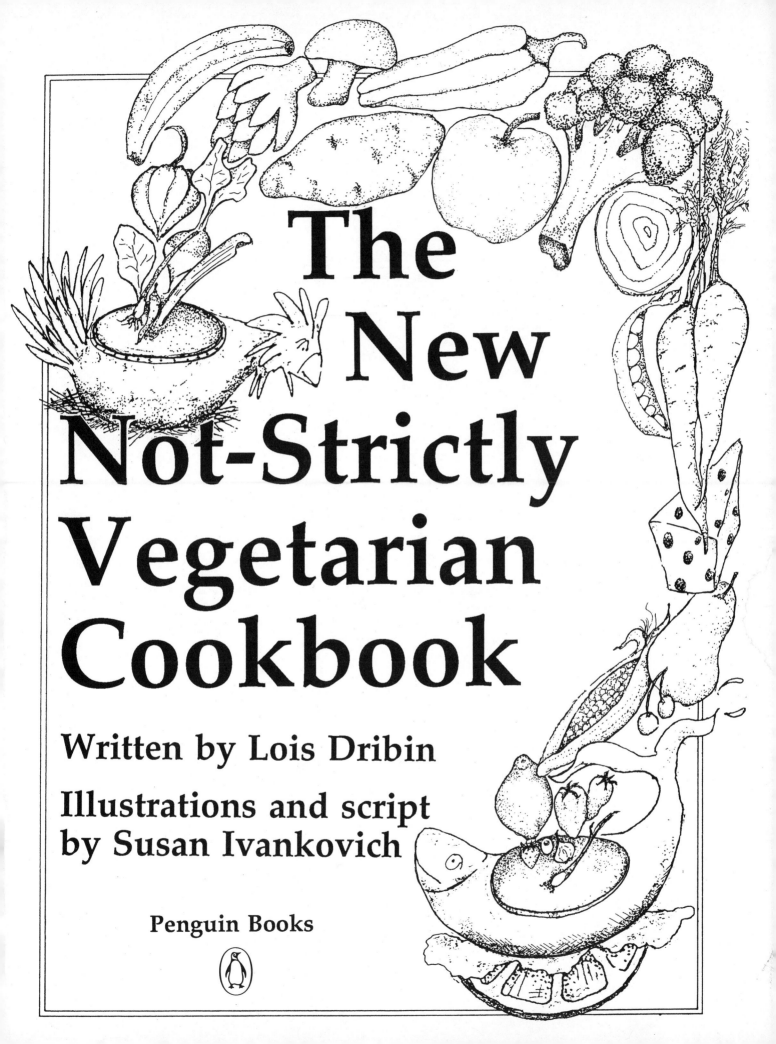

The New Not-Strictly Vegetarian Cookbook

Written by Lois Dribin

Illustrations and script
by Susan Ivankovich

Penguin Books

PENGUIN BOOKS
Published by the Penguin Group
Penguin Books USA Inc., 375 Hudson Street, New York, New York 10014, U.S.A.
Penguin Books Ltd, 27 Wrights Lane, London W8 5TZ, England
Penguin Books Australia Ltd, Ringwood, Victoria, Australia
Penguin Books Canada Ltd, 10 Alcorn Avenue, Toronto, Ontario, Canada M4V 3B2
Penguin Books (N.Z.) Ltd, 182–190 Wairau Road, Auckland 10, New Zealand

Penguin Books Ltd, Registered Offices: Harmondsworth, Middlesex, England

First published in Penguin Books 1995

1   3   5   7   9   10   8   6   4   2

ISBN 0 14 046.978 8
(CIP data available)

Printed in the United States of America

This book is dedicated, with love, to our children ... ♥ ♥ ♥

Rebecca Love, Sara Joy,
Matthew Dylan

Lois

Nash, Lindsey,
Megan, Jenna

Susan

<u>Acknowledgments</u>

With much gratitude and appreciation, we'd like to thank the following people who have helped make this book possible...

To all our dear friends and families for once again sharing their <u>best</u>.

To Richard, who always believed in the NSV... for his love, great sense of humor, moral support and invaluable literary input.

To Mike, for his never-ending support, love and friendship...

... and to both Mike and Jackie, who took over with Diamond Press, so this book could become a reality.

To our editor, Dawn Drzal, for her patience and for letting us do the book our way.

To our agent, Jane Dystel, who gave the New NSV its start.

And last, but not least, to all of you who bought and loved our first NSV.

Contents

Introduction

Well, here it is... 13 years later. The kids have grown and we have new names, extended families. Time sure has a way of passing. Life has been good and we're grateful.

Health and diet have certainly become an obsession in the 90s. We're sure you've heard it all: low-fat, high-fiber, vegetarianism, macrobiotics, just to name a few. Our heads are swimming with all the information we have received over the last several years, some valid, some contradictory.

We strongly feel that eating should be a pleasure and not a source of conflict and concern. Can we be blamed for loving butter? Is the right question really "Do we only live once?" Or "What about scalloped potatoes, Fettuccine Alfredo, Peking Duck, and chocolate mousse?" Let's face it... there's non-fat and then there's reality!

Of course we realize that we have to balance self-indulgence with self-discipline. Moderation is a word we have come to respect. We also recognize that more and more people have dietary restrictions, and nowadays it seems that there's a vegetarian in almost every family! Yet even though we have been cooking not-strictly vegetarian for years, we're at a loss when faced with recipes like Bulgur Wheat Germ Loaf! How can we relate? So what if it's good for you. Is that reason enough to eat it?

So here we are, trying to improve our diet without sacrificing our pleasure. That's what our book is all about. We offer healthful, unintimidating vegetarian choices as well as imaginative suggestions for cooking fish and poultry. We are not out to dazzle you with exotic recipes, complicated 15-step procedures or mysterious ingredients. Most of us simply do not have hours to spend in the kitchen. What with job, commuting, exercising and maintaining the rich cultural life of our children, life sometimes seems like a bizarre game of Beat the Clock!

This book is the fruit of many years of work... cooking, compiling the best recipes and, more recently, being chained to the drawing board for months at a time, racing to meet deadlines. Still, it has given us an opportunity to spend a lot more time together and to share many good laughs. It has been a great joy and pleasure... truly a labor of love, and we hope some of this spirit comes through to you.

Lois and Susan
Bucks County, Pennsylvania ~ 1995

Breakfast Ideas

Yucatán Yogurt Shake

From a little family-run restaurant on the Yucatán Peninsula in Mexico. Here is the original recipe, but use your imagination and try different fruits...melons... berries...peaches ∾ the perfect summer breakfast.

· SERVES 2 ·

1 pint plain yogurt
2 ripe bananas
1 ripe mango
1 ripe papaya
½ cup fresh pineapple
2 to 3 Tbsp. honey

Put it all into a blender or food processor and whirl into a smooth thick shake.

Serve immediately or chill... <u>very</u> refreshing.

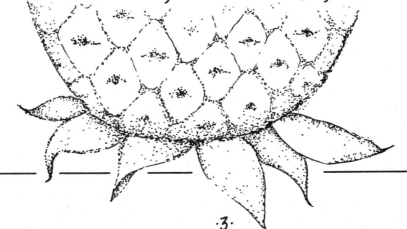

Jacquie's Veggie Eggs Benny

A real heart stopper... if you catch my drift. Steamed spinach or Nova Scotia smoked salmon can be used instead of avocado for a variation on a theme.

· SERVES 2 ·

* JACQUIE USES A DRIED HOLLANDAISE MADE BY MAYACAMAS... IT'S ALL NATURAL & CAN BE FOUND IN NATURAL FOOD AND GOURMET STORES.

   4 eggs, poached
   2 English muffins, split in half & toasted
   1 Haas avocado, peeled & sliced
 * 1 cup Hollandaise sauce (recipe follows)
   salt & pepper to taste

To poach eggs, fill a skillet with approximately 3" of water – bring to boil – crack eggs into water & simmer for about 5 minutes or till preferred done-ness. Meanwhile, make the Hollandaise sauce as directed & have it ready to go. Toast the muffins... place on plate with a few slices of avocado on each half. Place cooked eggs on top of each half and top with Hollandaise sauce, and a little salt & pepper... watch out!

Hollandaise Sauce

· MAKES 1 CUP ·

   ½ cup butter, melted   2 Tbsp. lemon juice
   3 egg yolks   ¼ tsp. salt

Melt butter in a small pot. Meanwhile, blend egg yolks, lemon juice & salt in a food processor or blender. Slowly add hot melted butter to egg yolks as you continue to blend.

Sherry's Granola

Wholesome and substantial... sticks to your ribs. Makes a lot so keep the bulk of it in an air-tight container in the freezer to prevent rancidity — very important! Thaws instantly.

· MAKES APPROXIMATELY 10 CUPS ·

1/4 cup sesame seeds
3/4 cup raw pumpkin seeds
6 cups quick cooking oats
1/4 cup unsweetened
    shredded coconut
3/4 cup maple syrup
3/4 cup raw cashews
3/4 cup walnuts

1/2 cup raw almonds
1/4 cup raw sunflower
        seeds
1 cup dried unsweetened
  pineapple, coarsely chopped
1/3 cup dried apples,
    coarsely chopped
2 cups raisins
1 cup raw wheat germ

Place sesame seeds and pumpkin seeds into a dry skillet. Toast on low till fragrant & golden. Remove from skillet & set aside. Mix oats, coconut & maple syrup together — place into same dry skillet & toast for approximately 10 minutes, stirring often. Remove from skillet & set aside. Place all of the seeds & nuts into a food processor, and process till coarsely chopped. Mix oats, chopped seeds & nuts together in a large bowl — add fruit and wheat germ and mix well.

Serve with milk or yogurt.

Jack's Banana Chip Muffins

Jack is a special guy with special needs — he came up with these delicious low-fat high-protein muffins after years of wild experimentation.

• MAKES 12 LARGE OR 24 SMALL MUFFINS •

1 cup soy flour
1 cup buckwheat flour
1 cup whole wheat pastry flour
} all three can be found at natural food stores

½ tsp. salt

1½ Tbsp. cinnamon

⅛ cup Dr. Bronner's Powdered Barley Malt or 1 cup Fruit Source (both found at natural food stores) or 1 cup sugar

3 Tbsp. baking powder

1 cup chopped pecans or walnuts

1 cup chocolate or carob chips

4 large ripe bananas, mashed (2 cups)

½ oz. butterbuds (look for in oils section at the market)

½ tsp. grated lemon rind

½ Tbsp. vanilla

4 egg whites, beaten

Preheat oven to 375°. Lightly oil 12 large or 24 small muffin cups (or use paper liners).

Mix the first 7 dry ingredients together in a

bowl. Add pecans and chocolate chips — mix well.

Mix mashed bananas, butterbuds, lemon rind and vanilla together well. Add to dry ingredients. Mix well, but do not overmix.

Beat egg whites till stiff — fold into batter. Fill muffin tins and "fire them up."

Bake at 375° for 25 minutes for large, and 20 minutes for small muffins.

Allow to cool a little — eat warm or at room temperature.

Mushroom and Zucchini Omelette

⌐ the name says it all !

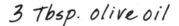

· MAKES 3 3-EGG OMELETTES ·

3 Tbsp. olive oil
1 small red onion, chopped
1 medium zucchini, chopped
½ lb. mushrooms, sliced
2 Tbsp. fresh chives, chopped

salt & pepper
9 large eggs
3 Tbsp. milk
3 Tbsp. butter
¼ lb. cheddar cheese, grated

Heat olive oil in a skillet ⌐ add onion & sauté 5 minutes. Add zucchini & sauté 5 minutes. Add mushrooms, chives, salt & pepper to taste ⌐ sauté 5 minutes. Remove from stove. Beat 3 eggs together in a bowl. Add 1 Tbsp. milk. Melt 1 Tbsp. butter in an omelette pan or small skillet & add eggs. Sprinkle with ⅓ of the cheddar cheese. Cook on a low heat till eggs set up (takes only minutes). Spoon ⅓ of the veggies onto the middle of the eggs....fold up the sides and try to slip the little devil out of the pan and onto a plate without destroying it! Repeat with remaining ingredients to make 2 more omelettes.

If you wish to serve all the omelettes together, then place the finished omelettes in a warm oven while making the rest.

Emma's Raspberry Muffins

Emma... so very young, yet quite the baker!

• YIELDS 18 MUFFINS •

2 cups unbleached white flour
½ tsp. salt
1 Tbsp. baking powder
1 cup sugar
2 medium eggs
6 Tbsp. butter, softened
1 tsp. almond extract
1 cup milk
¾ cup fresh raspberries (frozen O.K., but thaw & drain before using)

Preheat oven to 400° ¬ butter 18 muffin cups or use paper muffin liners (if you have un-used cups, put 1" water in each one). Mix *first three ingredients* in a bowl & set aside. Beat sugar, eggs & butter together. Add almond extract & milk. Mix. Slowly add dry ingredients to wet ingredients ¬ mix well, but do not over-mix. Gently mix raspberries into batter ¬ spoon batter into muffin tins.

Bake at 400° for 15 to 20 minutes. Serve warm or at room temperature... or toasted with butter and jam. ♡ ♡ ♡ ♡ ♡ ♡ ♡ ♡ ♡ ♡ ♡ ♡

<u>Veggie Omelette</u>

You can't begin to imagine how difficult it is to keep coming up with names for all these recipes. This title may not be creative... but it's certainly not misleading!

·MAKES 2 LARGE 3-EGG OMELETTES·

1 Tbsp. olive oil
½ red bell pepper, chopped
½ large sweet Vidalia onion, chopped
    (if Vidalias aren't available, use a red onion)
1 small zucchini, chopped
3 large Swiss chard leaves, chopped
1 large ripe tomato, chopped
1 Tbsp. fresh sweet marjoram, chopped

6 X-large eggs, beaten
2 Tbsp. milk
salt & pepper to taste
2 Tbsp. butter
¼ lb. Provolone cheese, thinly sliced

Heat oil in a skillet ~ add red pepper & onion ~ sauté 5 minutes. Add zucchini & chard ~ sauté 5 more minutes. Add tomato & marjoram ~ sauté 1 minutes. Remove from skillet & set aside.

Beat 3 of the 6 eggs together in a bowl with 1

Tbsp. milk and some salt & pepper. Melt 1 of the 2 Tbsp. butter in an omelette pan or small skillet. Pour eggs into pan, and lay half of the Provolone cheese slices on top of the eggs. Cook on low heat for 3-5 minutes, or till it sets up. Spoon ½ of the veggies into center of eggs ~ fold sides over top and remove from pan.

Repeat the process again with the remaining 3 eggs and veggies.

Serve with a good Russian black bread.

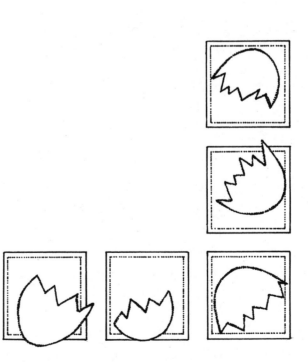

Annie's Blueberry Coffee Cake

Serve with breakfast or as dessert ~ warm ~ with whipped cream.

· MAKES A 10" TUBE PAN CAKE·

TOPPING:
- $\frac{1}{2}$ cup sugar
- $\frac{1}{3}$ cup flour
- $\frac{1}{2}$ tsp. cinnamon
- $\frac{1}{4}$ cup butter or margarine

CAKE:
- $\frac{3}{4}$ cup sugar
- $\frac{1}{4}$ cup butter or margarine
- 1 egg
- $\frac{1}{2}$ cup milk
- 2 cups flour
- 2 tsp. baking powder
- $\frac{1}{2}$ tsp. salt
- 2 cups blueberries (fresh or frozen)

Preheat oven to 375°. Butter & flour a 10" tube pan. If using frozen blueberries, thaw slightly & blot off moisture. Set aside. Place topping ingredients into a bowl & blend with a pastry blender till crumbly ~ set aside. Mix sugar, butter & egg together in a large bowl ~ add milk & mix well. Combine dry ingredients together in another bowl & add to batter. Mix well. Carefully blend in blueberries. Pour batter into buttered tube pan. Sprinkle topping evenly over top. Bake 45-50 minutes.

Mexican Cornbread
Olé!

· SERVES 6-8 ·

4 large eggs
½ cup canola oil
2 cups canned diced chilies
1 17-oz. can creamed corn
1 cup buttermilk
⅔ cup turbinado sugar
½ tsp. salt
2 cups cornmeal
1 cup unbleached white flour
4 tsp. baking powder

Preheat oven to 325°. Oil a large baking dish. Beat eggs with oil in a large bowl. Add chilies, corn, and buttermilk. Mix well.

In another bowl mix sugar, salt, cornmeal, flour and baking powder together.

Add the dry ingredients to egg mixture. Mix well & spoon into oiled baking dish.

Bake at 325° for 40 minutes. Serve warm.

Huevos Rancheros

For a special breakfast or brunch. About the refried beans...
I use an excellent instant refried, made by Fantastic Food.
They are seasoned well and the best thing about them is that
they are dried and only need the addition of water to recon-
stitute them.

· SERVES 2 ·

4 6" flour tortillas
1 cup refried beans
1 Tbsp. butter
4 large eggs
1 cup grated cheddar or jack cheese
½ to 1 cup salsa
½ to 1 cup sour cream
¼ cup fresh cilantro, chopped

Place tortillas in a warm oven to heat. Make refried
beans as directed or get ready to open the jar. Melt
butter in a large skillet & crack eggs into skillet
(it should hold all 4 eggs). Sprinkle with cheese ↵
Cover & cook about 5 to 7 minutes till cheese is
melted & eggs are cooked (with yolks slightly loose).
Spread refried beans onto the warmed tortillas, remove eggs from pan & place 1 on each tortilla. Top
with a generous amount of salsa, a little sour cream,
and garnish with chopped cilantro.

Buttermilk Biscuits

Down-home comfort food — a perfect match for most soups & stews.

• MAKES 1 DOZEN BISCUITS •

2 cups unbleached white flour (plus ¼ cup for kneading)
3 tsp. baking powder
1 tsp. baking soda
¼ tsp. mace (optional)
½ tsp. salt
4 Tbsp. butter, melted
1 egg
1 cup buttermilk

Preheat oven to 350°. Mix dry ingredients together in a large bowl. Melt butter on low heat. In a large bowl beat egg, butter and buttermilk together. Add the dry ingredients, mixing with a wooden spoon. Do not over-mix.

Turn onto a floured surface & knead 3 minutes until smooth. Cut the dough in half. Set the other half aside. Roll out to about ½" thick. Using a glass, a round or heart-shaped cookie cutter, cut out biscuits. Repeat with remaining dough. Place onto a lightly buttered cookie sheet. Bake at 350° for 15 minutes. Serve warm.

Har's Home Fries

First he brought us Har's Holes-In-One... now he brings us his home fries. He's quite the breakfast kind of a guy!

· SERVES 4 ·

8 medium red potatoes
¼ cup canola oil
½ onion, chopped
½ green pepper, chopped
1 Tbsp. dried dill

1 tsp. dried parsley
1 tsp. dried basil
1 Tbsp. paprika
salt & pepper to taste
1 Tbsp. gomasio

Place potatoes in a pot — cover with water — bring to a boil. As soon as they start to boil, remove from heat & pour into a colander to drain. Let them sit 5 minutes.

Heat oil in a skillet and add potatoes. Fry on medium/ high heat for 5 minutes, flipping with a spatula to coat well with oil. Add onion and pepper. Cook another 5 minutes, continuing to flip as you go. Add herbs and a little salt... cook and flip another 5 minutes.

Remove from heat — add a little black pepper and some gomasio — serve.

Barbara's Over-Stuffed Coffee Cake Muffins

Barbara, the owner/chef of the Little Italian Cookie Company in Portland, Oregon, says that these fruit-filled breakfast muffins are her best seller.

· MAKES 12 LARGE MUFFINS ·

STREUSEL TOPPING:
6 oz. butter
1¼ cups sugar
1 cup flour

FRUIT:
3 apples, pears or peaches –
  peeled, cored & thinly sliced
     OR
2 cups fresh blueberries,
  raspberries, strawberries
  or cranberries

MUFFINS:
3 cups flour
1¼ cups sugar
2 tsp. baking powder
½ tsp. salt
3 eggs, beaten
½ cup milk
½ cup sour cream
1 cup canola oil

Preheat oven to 375°. Oil 12 muffin cups (or use paper liners). Make topping: melt butter in a small pot on low heat. Remove from heat. Add sugar & flour, & mix well with a fork till crumbly. Set aside. Prepare the fruit, place in a bowl & set aside. Mix all dry ingredients together in a bowl. Mix all wet ingredients together in another bowl. Add wet ingredients to dry – mix well. Fill muffin cups ¾ full & stuff 4 or 5 slices of fruit or 2 Tbsp. berries into batter. Sprinkle streusel topping over each muffin. Bake at 375° for 25 to 30 minutes.

Salads &

Salad Dressings

Thai Salad Dressing

An unusual dressing for Thai Vegetable Salad or Thai Grilled Chicken Salad, and... oh yes... it's totally void of fat!

· DRESSES A LARGE SALAD ·

1 red bell pepper, coarsely chopped
2 cloves garlic, coarsely chopped
juice of 2 limes
juice of 2 lemons
2 Tbsp. fish sauce or tamari
¼ tsp. hot red pepper flakes (optional)

Place all the above ingredients into a blender or food processor and whirl.

Ilse's Oriental Salad Dressing

A winner - great on greens, Oriental pasta salads, tofu, fish, chicken... anything!

· MAKES ENOUGH FOR 2 SALADS ·

2 Tbsp. canola oil
6 Tbsp. tamari
6 Tbsp. rice vinegar
    (sweetened)

2 Tbsp. roasted sesame oil
1 tsp. hot Szechuan chili paste
1½ tsp. brown sugar

Mix it all together well & use your imagination!

Myra's Zesty Lemon Salad Dressing

Very lemony with a hint of mint ~ great on a summer salad.

· MAKES OVER A CUP OF DRESSING·

½ cup lemon juice
½ cup extra-virgin olive oil
1 tsp. tamari
2 cloves garlic, pressed
1 Tbsp. Dijon mustard
1 mint leaf

Mix all ingredients together & use as needed. Keep extra in the refrigerator.

Penny's Salad Dressing

· MAKES OVER 1½ CUPS OF DRESSING ~ A CRUET-FULL

1 cup balsamic vinegar
½ cup extra-virgin olive oil
1 Tbsp. Dijon mustard
2 cloves garlic, pressed
1 tsp. dried marjoram
1 tsp. dried basil

Put all of the above ingredients into a blender & blend for a few seconds. Keep extra in the refrigerator.

Coleslaw

Refreshing and brightly colored ~ quite a happy little slaw!

· SERVES MANY ·

1 small head green cabbage, shredded
1 small head red cabbage, shredded
3 large carrots, grated
3 Tbsp. apple cider vinegar
2 Tbsp. raw sugar
salt & pepper to taste
1 cup mayonnaise

If you have a food processor, for heaven's sake use it. If not, shred cabbages on the large side of a four-sided grater. So, in other words, shred and grate cabbages and carrots however you would go about it!

Place into a large bowl ~ add remaining ingredients. Mix well and serve at room temperature or chilled.

Thai Cucumber Salad

Great with any Thai meal... a must with Thai Fish Cakes.

· SERVES 4-6 ·

3 medium seeded cucumbers, peeled (if not
                organic) and chopped
½ cup red onion, chopped
¼ cup boiling water
1 Tbsp. sugar
¼ tsp. salt (or to taste)
a few hot red pepper flakes (optional)
½ cup rice vinegar
½ cup roasted peanuts, shelled & coarsely chopped
2 Tbsp. fresh cilantro, chopped

Place cucumbers and onion in a bowl, and mix. Set aside.

Mix boiling water with sugar and salt in a small bowl. Add hot pepper flakes and vinegar — mix well.

Pour over veggies — add peanuts and mix.

Garnish with fresh cilantro — serve at room temperature.

Julie's Roasted Garlic Salad

Divine!

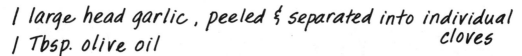

· SERVES 4-6 ·

1 large head garlic, peeled & separated into individual
1 Tbsp. olive oil   cloves

2 bunches arugula, washed & broken into bite-size pieces

1 large head red leaf lettuce, washed & broken into
                                                    bite-size pieces

2 small cucumbers, peeled & cut into thin rounds
                        (leave skins on if organic)

1 8-oz. jar marinated artichoke hearts, cut into pieces
                                        (discard oil)

8 sun-dried tomatoes, packed in oil ~ drained & cut
                                        into strips

¼ lb. freshly grated Asiago cheese

<u>Dressing</u> :
    ¼ cup olive oil
    ⅛ cup balsamic vinegar
    2 Tbsp. Kikkoman teriyaki sauce

Preheat oven to 350°. Put garlic cloves in a bowl & drizzle with
1 Tbsp. olive oil. Mix. Place in small pan or roaster with lid
(or cover with foil). Bake for 30 minutes. Remove cover and
bake 15 more minutes. Remove from oven & let cool as you
make the salad. Place arugula, lettuce, cukes, artichokes &
sun-dried tomatoes in large salad bowl & toss. Make dressing
by mixing all dressing ingredients together in a bowl or
cruet. Mix well & pour over salad. Add garlic cloves and
sprinkle with cheese. Toss and serve.

Thai Vegetable Salad

A glorious green salad with peanuts and a lime dressing —

· SERVES 4 ·

½ head green cabbage, shredded
½ head red cabbage, shredded
2 carrots, grated
1 head romaine lettuce, washed and coarsely chopped
2 large ripe tomatoes, sliced
2 cucumbers, sliced
1 cup dry roasted unsalted peanuts
½ cup fresh cilantro, chopped (optional)

In a large salad bowl, combine all the veggies. Add peanuts and cilantro. Toss well.

Dress with Thai Salad Dressing — see pg. 21 — toss and serve.

Thai Grilled Chicken Salad

A very unique salad... can be served as a main course on a hot summer night with a cold glass of Thai beer.

· SERVES 4 ·

2 lbs. boneless chicken breasts

MARINADE:
1 Tbsp. canola oil
1 Tbsp. tamari
juice of 1 lime
¼ cup cilantro, chopped

SALAD:
1 head romaine lettuce, washed & chopped
2 large ripe tomatoes, sliced
1 cucumber, sliced
1 red onion, sliced
½ cup cilantro, chopped

THAI SALAD DRESSING ... (see pg. 21)

Mix marinade ingredients together in a bowl & pour over chicken. Marinate for at least 2 hours in the fridge. Remove from fridge while you prepare the grill. Grill chicken 7-10 minutes on each side. Let cool as you prepare the rest of the salad & dressing. Make Thai Salad Dressing as directed. Divide the lettuce up & place on 4 dinner plates. Add tomato, cucumber, and onion. Cut the chicken into bite-size pieces, and divide evenly on top of each of the 4 plates. Shake up the dressing and pour over each individual salad. Serve.

Japanese Ginger Salad Dressing

Try this dressing on a bowl of greens to accompany Grilled Salmon and Chilled Sesame Soba Noodles.

• MAKES ENOUGH TO DRESS A LARGE SALAD •

2 Tbsp. roasted sesame seeds
2 Tbsp. safflower oil
2 Tbsp. roasted sesame oil
3 Tbsp. tamari
juice of 1 large lemon
1 Tbsp. freshly grated ginger

To roast sesame seeds, place in a dry skillet and heat on low until they turn golden ~ mixing a little as they are browning. This takes only a few minutes, so watch carefully to prevent burning.

Place remaining ingredients into a cruet ~ shake well. Dress salad ~ sprinkle some sesame seeds on top ~ toss well and serve.

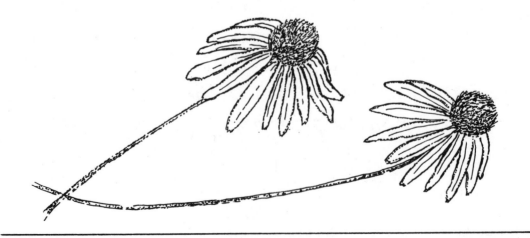

Garlicky Croutons

Homemade croutons are really special — they are easy to make, and can be kept fresh in the freezer to use when needed... for a bowl of greens, soups, stews & pastas.

• MAKES A TON •

1 large day-old French or Italian bread, cut into cubes

3 large cloves garlic, pressed
4 Tbsp. olive oil
¼ tsp. dried oregano
¼ tsp. dried basil
Salt & pepper

Place the bread cubes into a large bowl. Add garlic and drizzle with olive oil. Sprinkle with herbs, salt and pepper. Mix well. Spread onto a cookie sheet.

Bake at 300° for 30 minutes.

Roasted Seeds and Nuts

Roasted seeds & nuts are very nutritious and are a good source of protein. Their roasted flavor and crunchy texture add much to salads, vegetables, rice & pasta dishes. Sometimes I roast one or two kinds while at other times I mix quite a few varieties together.

It is best to roast only as much as you plan to use right away, as roasting tends to make seeds and nuts rancid quicker. If you should have more than needed for 1 day, place the remaining nuts in an air-tight container, refrigerate, and use as soon as possible.

The following is a list of the ones I use most often, along with the instructions for roasting...

Sesame Seeds	Peanuts
Pumpkin Seeds	Almonds
Pine Nuts	Walnuts
Sunflower Seeds	Pecans

To roast, place the seeds and/or nuts in a dry skillet. Roast over a medium heat for a few minutes, or until they start to have a fragrant aroma and are golden brown.
Stir as you are roasting and stay close by, as they take only minutes to brown and it is easy to burn them.
Remove from heat and allow to cool a few minutes.

Blue Cheese Vinaigrette

Makes enough to dress a very large salad — or refrigerate what you don't use and enjoy another time.

¼ cup olive oil
¼ cup apple cider vinegar
(or red wine vinegar or
balsamic vinegar)
1 clove garlic, pressed
¼ tsp. salt
black pepper
2 oz. blue cheese

In a bowl, place olive oil, vinegar, garlic, and salt & pepper.
Crumble blue cheese into the bowl and mix well.
Serve over your favorite bowl of greens.

Oil and Vinegar

A simple oil and vinegar dressing is without a doubt my favorite dressing for a fresh bowl of greens. Often I stray and try others, but I always go back to good old oil and vinegar.

It is difficult to give an exact recipe for this dressing, as it depends on how large a salad you are serving. It tends to be one of those things you just get a feel for.

- salt & pepper
- extra-virgin olive oil
- red wine vinegar (or balsamic or apple cider vinegar)

What I do is prepare my salad in a large bowl, then I sprinkle a little salt & pepper over top. Then I pour the olive oil evenly over the greens, and then a little of the vinegar. Then, toss well & serve immediately.

Start out with a small amount of oil and vinegar, toss it, and taste it to see if more is needed — rather than using too much too soon.

Cucumber and Tomato Salad

I make this salad often in the summer when my garden is producing cukes and tomatoes faster than the speed of light!

· SERVES 4-6 ·

4 smallish cucumbers ~ cut into thin rounds
   (leave skins on if organic.... otherwise peel)
4 large ripe tomatoes, chopped
1 small red onion, thinly sliced
3 Tbsp. olive oil
4 Tbsp. apple cider vinegar
salt & pepper to taste

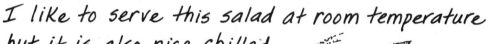

Place veggies into bowl ~ add oil, vinegar, and salt & pepper to taste. Mix well and serve.

I like to serve this salad at room temperature but it is also nice chilled.

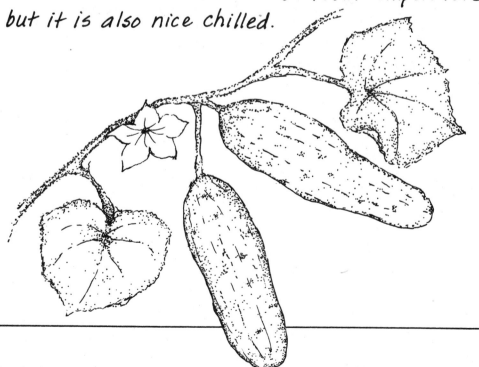

Caesar Salad

Does anyone really know why Caesar Salad was thus named?? Was it Julius' favorite bowl of greens, or what!!

·SERVES 4·

1 large head romaine lettuce
2 large cloves garlic, pressed
juice of 1 large lemon
4 Tbsp. extra-virgin olive oil
1 Tbsp. apple cider vinegar
1 Tbsp. Dijon mustard
1 squirt of anchovy paste (optional)
freshly ground pepper
¼ cup freshly grated Parmesan cheese
homemade croutons (recipe follows)

Rinse lettuce under cold water – use a salad spinner or shake out excess water, and wrap lettuce in a clean cotton dish towel and chill.

To make dressing: Mix garlic, lemon, olive oil, vinegar, mustard, anchovy paste & black pepper in a large salad bowl. Cut or break the lettuce into bite-size pieces, and place in the bowl with the dressing. Toss to coat well. Add cheese and croutons – mix well and serve immediately.

Homemade Croutons

~ beats the commercial brands tenfold ... very easy

Day-old French or Italian bread
Olive oil

Cut bread into bite-size cubes. Sprinkle with a little olive oil. Place on a cookie sheet & bake for ½ hour in a 350° oven.

THE MISSING RAW EGG STORY...

Traditionally Caesar Salad has been made with a raw or coddled yolk. However, there has been an increase in Salmonella (we've always wanted to go to a Halloween party as SAM & ELLA ... you know, break down those barriers with a little humor!), caused by the consumption of raw egg. So, as far as we're concerned, the raw egg is out totally. If you insist, you can coddle the egg by placing the raw egg in a pot of water, and as soon as the water starts to boil, remove egg, separate by dis-carding the white & use the coddled yolk. Good luck!

Sweet Balsamic Vinaigrette

• MAKES A LITTLE OVER A CUP •

½ cup extra-virgin olive oil
1 tsp. sugar
½ cup balsamic vinegar
1 large clove garlic, pressed
salt & pepper to taste

Place all of the above ingredients into a cruet, and shake well. Serve.

Ken's Salad Dressing

⌐ the glaze-Meister

• MAKES 1 CUP •

⅔ cup canola oil
4 Tbsp. balsamic vinegar
3 dashes roasted sesame oil
4 tsp. Dijon mustard

2 Tbsp. brown sugar
⅓ cup water
1 tsp. garlic powder
1 tsp. black pepper

Just mix all ingredients together well and use.

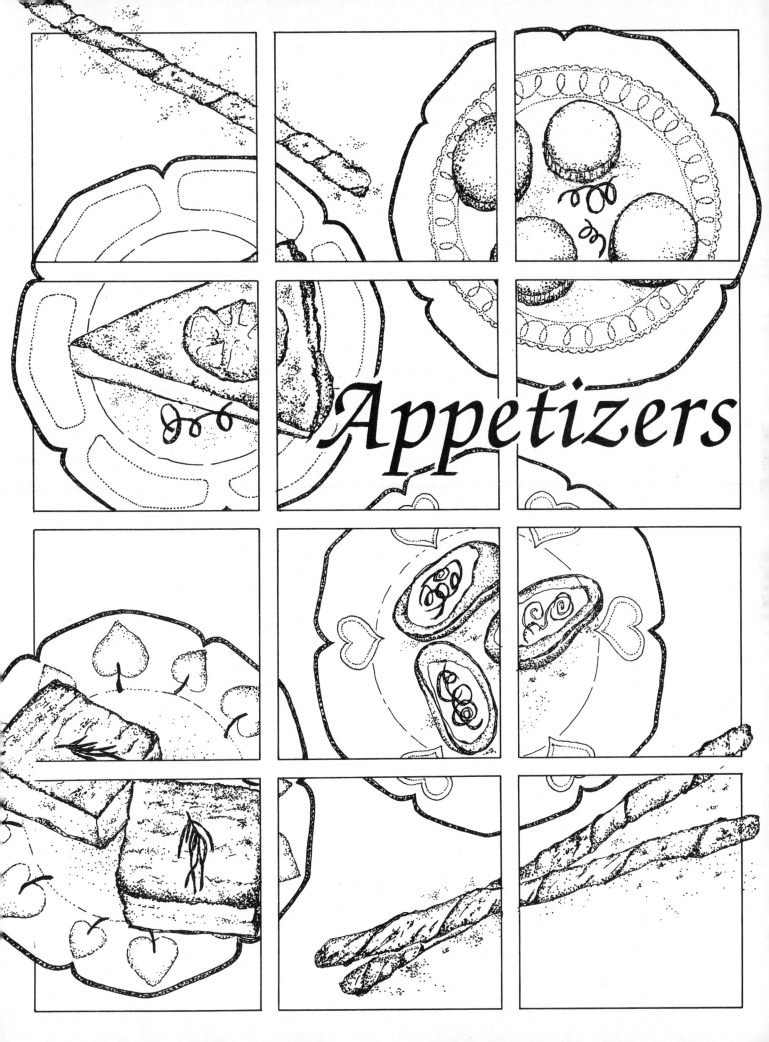

Appetizers

Sam's Infamous Salsa

· MAKES 3-4 CUPS ·

12 plum tomatoes, chopped
½ cup onion, chopped
1 clove garlic, pressed
1 cup cilantro, chopped
2 jalapeno peppers, chopped
(use seeds if you like it real hot)
juice of 1 large lemon
1 Tbsp. olive oil
½ tsp. cumin powder
salt & black pepper to taste
(Sam uses about ¾ tsp. salt)

Mix all the above ingredients together in a bowl.
Chill or serve at room temperature with tortilla
chips.

Pickled Beets

Another one of those recipes almost too simple to mention; however, it's a favorite at our house. Beets are high in fiber and are loaded with vitamins and minerals.

• SERVES 4-6 (make more as they keep forever in the fridge) •

> 2 bunches of beets
>   (about 10-12 large ones)
> Water to cover
> Salt to taste
> ⅔ cup apple cider vinegar

The easiest way to cook beets is to cut off the tops and bottoms close to the beet. Put in a pot & cover with water. Cover and bring to a boil. Reduce heat to medium and boil for 20 minutes, or till tender firm when pierced with a fork.
Remove from heat, drain in a colander, and let cool for ½ hour. With your hands, slip the peel off the beet and rinse under cold water.
Slice beets into rounds ~ place in a bowl and add salt and vinegar. Mix well and chill at least one hour. Mix again before serving.

Baba Ghanouj

In an effort to spell correctly, I have been diligently using a dictionary whilst writing this book. Was I ever surprised to find the correct spelling of Baba Ghanouj. Had I not looked it up I would certainly have spelled it Baba Ganosh. Who would have thought?! About the Baba... once a Lebanese woman complimented my Baba. She said that it had a wonderful smokey flavor. Little did she know that the smokey flavor wasn't intentional... I just baked the eggplants till they were very soft! So... for whatever it's worth, here's how I did it.

· YIELDS APPROXIMATELY 2 CUPS ·

2 large eggplants (when baked they shrink like crazy!)
2 large cloves garlic, pressed
3 Tbsp. tahini
Juice of 2 lemons
3 Tbsp. olive oil
salt to taste

Preheat oven to 350°. Place whole eggplants on a cookie sheet & make a long slit on the top of each one. Bake at 350° for 1 hour. Remove from oven & let cool for ½ hour. Scoop inside of eggplant out of skin & place in a food processor or blender ~ add remaining ingredients & whirl till smooth. Serve at room temperature, or chilled with warm pita bread.

A Fennel Appetizer

Fennel is a fine-tasting vegetable served raw or cooked. Its subtle anise flavor and crunchy texture are unbeatable ...
  ... and PRESTO, it takes minutes to prepare!

Serve alongside sun-dried tomatoes, roasted peppers, an array of cheeses & some good breads.

· SERVES 4 ·

    2 large fennel bulbs, sliced
    olive oil
    herb salt, or salt & pepper

Place fennel slices on a plate and drizzle with a little olive oil. Sprinkle a little herb salt or salt & pepper on top & serve.

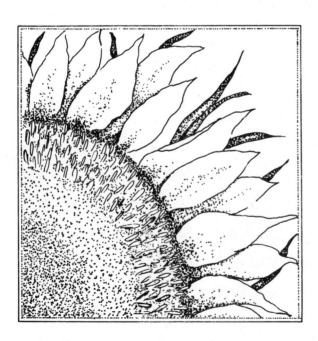

Fast Hummus

I used to believe that the only way to make hummus was to start from scratch, soaking the chick peas overnight and cooking the little devils for hours. Nice idea, but nothing beats opening a can of already cooked beans and starting from there. With a good food processor or blender you're practically home free!

· YIELDS 2 CUPS ·

1 15-oz. can of chick peas (garbanzo beans)
3 large cloves garlic
2 Tbsp. tahini
juice of 1 large lemon
3 Tbsp. olive oil
1 tsp. ground cumin (optional)
salt to taste (I find that if the chick peas are packed in salted water, additional salt is not necessary)
paprika

Okay, here goes... put all of the above ingredients into a food processor or blender, and whirl till you have a smooth paste.

Spoon into a bowl, sprinkle with a little paprika and serve with fresh warmed pita bread.

Roasted Peppers with Pine Nuts & Raisins

A great starter piled onto slices of sour-dough bread. If you can't relate to the raisins, then just leave them out... but I think they provide an interesting contrast.

·SERVES 4-8·

6 large red bell peppers
⅓ cup pine nuts
⅓ cup golden or regular raisins
½ cup Sweet Balsamic Vinaigrette (see pg. 36)

To roast peppers – place whole peppers on a broiling pan. Put in oven about 4 inches from the top broiler flame. Broil about 7 to 10 minutes or until the tops of the peppers are charred black. Turn peppers over & char the other side. Continue flipping till all sides are charred. Remove from oven & place peppers into a large brown bag. Close the bag up tightly & let peppers rest ½ hour. This allows the peppers to steam a bit while cooling, which helps the skins to slide off easily. While the peppers are in the bag cooling, make Sweet Balsamic Vinaigrette (pg. 36).

Remove peppers from bag. Peel off skin with hands – cut open and remove stems & seeds. Cut into strips & place in a bowl. Add pine nuts, raisins & vinaigrette. Mix well. Refrigerate until ready to serve.

Skordalia

Skordalia is a rather intense but quite delicious Greek dip or paste. Try it with Pickled Beets or serve it with grilled fish.

· SERVES 4 ·

1 cup walnuts
2 large cloves garlic
¼ cup olive oil
juice of 1 lemon
salt to taste

Put all the above ingredients into a food processor or blender ... and purée.

Serve at room temperature.

Roasted Garlic

For garlic lovers, roasted garlic is nectar from the gods!
Roasting transforms the garlic ... the flavor mellows,
becoming sweet yet pungent ... the texture changes completely, taking on the consistency of butter or a soft
cheese — making it marvelously spreadable.

Just think ... no cholesterol ... scrumptious ... and you
can slather as much as you want on bread, and grow
thinner as you eat it !!

  1 whole head of garlic

To roast — peel off any excess papery cover-
ings from the whole head of garlic, but leave
the garlic head intact, with the peel left on.
                    — (does that make sense?)
Place the garlic head onto a little baking pan,
and bake 1 hour in a 350° oven.

Remove from oven and allow to cool 10 minutes.
Break off a clove and squeeze out the softened
garlic onto a slice of bread. It's nice topped
with a roasted pepper, some Brie cheese, sun-
dried tomatoes ... let your imagination
                                    run
                                    wild !!

Sun-Dried Tomato & Pepper Sandwich

Enjoy this sandwich alone... or with a friend ⁓ or, cut it up and share with many friends.

1 large loaf of French or Italian bread
3 Tbsp. olive oil
2 large cloves of garlic, pressed
1 red bell pepper, sliced
6 sun-dried tomatoes ⁓ packed in oil ⁓ drain and cut into strips
¼ lb. mozzarella cheese, grated
2 Tbsp. balsamic vinegar
1 small bunch arugula leaves, rinsed

Preheat oven to 325°. Cut bread in half length-wise, and set aside. Heat oil in skillet ⁓ add garlic, pepper and sun-dried tomatoes. Sauté 10 minutes till peppers are soft-ish.

Open bread up, flatten, and sprinkle evenly with cheese. Drizzle with balsamic vinegar. Add arugula leaves ⁓ add sautéed sun-dried tomatoes and pepper, and close up bread. Wrap up in aluminum foil and place in oven. Bake for 15 minutes... remove from foil... let cool a few minutes and serve.

Mango Chutney

Boy, was I groping in the dark when I made this chutney! It was inspired by a mango chutney my friend Julie made — but I added several other ingredients. It's great with grilled chicken or fish.

The following recipe was made for a party & serves 20 people, so cut it in half or so if making for fewer folks.

· SERVES 20 ·

10 very ripe mangoes, peeled & chopped
juice of 3 limes
1 cup raisins
½ large red onion, finely chopped
3 Tbsp. olive oil
2 Tbsp. Tabasco sauce
2 Tbsp. freshly grated ginger
1 cup freshly chopped cilantro
¼ cup freshly chopped mint

Mix all of the above ingredients together in a bowl. Cover and refrigerate 2 to 3 hours before serving.

Roasted Peppers

Roasting peppers takes a little time and effort, but is well worth it. Commercial jarred peppers don't compare. Serve them with anchovies, fresh mozzarella cheese & sun-dried tomatoes. Use in sandwiches, salads, pasta dishes, omelettes... you name it!

· MAKES A LOT ·

12 red, yellow or orange bell peppers
3 cloves garlic, pressed
¼ cup olive oil
salt

Preheat the broiler. Place peppers onto a broiling pan, and broil 4-6" from top broiler flame or heat. Cook until the skins are black. Turn the peppers to blacken skins all over.

Transfer peppers to a brown paper bag ~ close the bag up tight, and allow the peppers to cool and steam in the bag for 20 to 30 minutes. Remove... peel off skins... remove stem and seeds.

Place peppers in a bowl, and add garlic, olive oil and salt to taste. Mix well. Chill before serving.

Julie's Black Bean Pile-Up

Julie is a great, creative cook — but she refuses to admit it. This is something she often makes when she has left-over cooked corn-on-the-cob. ♡

· SERVES 4-6 ·

2 15-oz. cans of black beans
Kernels from 2 ears cooked corn-on-the-cob
2 Tbsp. olive oil
juice of 1 lemon
½ tsp. ground cumin
½ tsp. chili powder
salt & pepper
½ Vidalia onion, chopped (if Vidalias aren't available, use red onion)
1 medium red bell pepper, chopped
¾ cup of good salsa, mild or hot
4 Tbsp. real sour cream
1 ripe avocado, sliced into strips

Pour beans into a large decorative bowl. Spoon corn kernels over beans. Now, take 1 Tbsp. olive oil & ½ lemon, and drizzle over corn & beans. Sprinkle with ¼ tsp. of the chili and ¼ tsp. of cumin, and a little salt & pepper. Add chopped onion and red pepper. Pour salsa around the outside edge of beans, corn, etc.

Now... here's the tricky part, and I'm sure that only Julie would think of doing this...
Take two fingers and place in the center of the beans and things, and move them in a small clockwise direction, continuing until there's a large hole in the middle. Fill the hole with the sour cream.
Place the avocado strips in a fan-like arrangement around the opening. Drizzle the rest of the olive oil and lemon juice over everything. Then sprinkle with remaining chili, cumin, and a little salt & pepper.
Serve with warm tortillas.

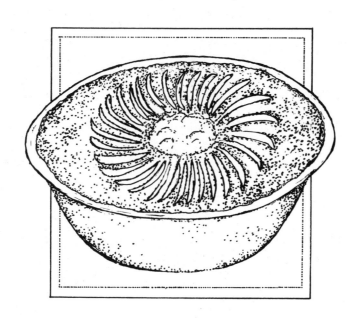

Cucumber Raita

⌐ a cool, soothing ally to a spicy Indian meal

· SERVES 4-6 ·

2 cucumbers
2 cups plain yogurt
1 tsp. ground cumin
salt to taste

Peel and grate cucumbers. Place in a bowl,
and add yogurt, cumin and a little salt.
Mix well and serve.

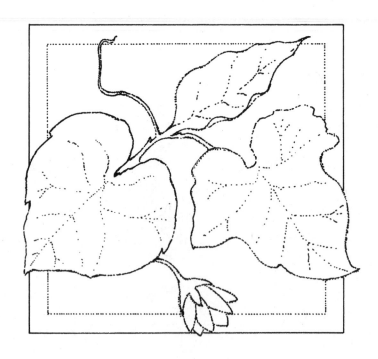

Soups

Mushroom Barley Soup

An old favorite...look for hulled barley at health food stores — it is the most nutritious form of the grain as only its outer husk has been removed.

· MAKES A GOOD SIZE POT OF SOUP - FEEDS UP TO 8 ·

2 Tbsp. butter or olive oil
1 large onion, chopped
2 cloves garlic, pressed
½ cup fresh parsley, chopped
2 Tbsp. fresh thyme, chopped
1 lb. mushrooms, sliced
2 carrots, chopped
1 yam, peeled & chopped
1 cup hulled barley — rinse well
2 cups chicken or vegetable broth
8 cups water
salt & pepper to taste

Melt butter in a large soup pot. Add onion and garlic — sauté 5 minutes. Add parsley, thyme and mushrooms — sauté 5 minutes. Add carrots, yam, barley, broth and water. Cover & bring to a boil. Reduce heat to low and simmer for 2 hours, stirring often.
Add salt & pepper to taste before serving.

Elise's Gazpacho

Elise adds cilantro in place of parsley for all of us cilantro lovers — but parsley can be used for all of you cilantro haters!

· SERVES 4 ·

3 ripe tomatoes, quartered
½ cup onion, coarsely chopped
½ cup red pepper, coarsely chopped
½ cup cucumber, coarsely chopped
1 tsp. salt
2 cloves garlic, chopped
¼ tsp. black pepper
¼ tsp. Tabasco sauce
1½ tsp. Worcestershire sauce
1 Tbsp. olive oil
2 Tbsp. lemon juice
3 fresh basil leaves (optional)
¾ cup V-8 juice
¼ cup cilantro, coarsely chopped

Place all of the above ingredients into a food processor or blender. Whirl till blended — do not purée ... it should be slightly chunky.

Chill before serving.

New Manhattan Clam Chowder

This hearty chowder is a cross between New England + Manhattan clam chowders... hence the name. It's pink in color and is quite scrumptious.

• SERVES 6-8 •

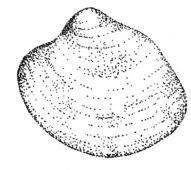

3 Tbsp. butter
1 large Spanish onion, chopped
1 large clove garlic, pressed
2 carrots, chopped
3 celery ribs, chopped
6 small red potatoes, chopped
½ cup fresh parsley, chopped
1 quart fresh minced clams, juice and all
                    (ask for them at the fish market)
1 2-lb. can crushed tomatoes
8 cups water
¼ cup sherry
2 Tbsp. Chesapeake Bay seasoning
1 cup Half & Half
salt & pepper to taste

Melt butter in a heavy-bottom soup pot. Add onion & garlic. Sauté 5 minutes. Add carrots, celery, potatoes & parsley – sauté 5 minutes. Add clams, tomatoes & water. Cover and bring to a boil – reduce heat & simmer 20 minutes. Add sherry, Chesapeake Bay seasoning, Half & Half, and salt & pepper. Mix well – cover & simmer 10 minutes. Serve.

French Lentil Soup

French lentils are different from the common brown lentils. They are small & delicate, and are often seen wearing a beret!

· SERVES 6-8 ·

4 Tbsp. olive oil
1 onion, chopped
3 large cloves garlic, pressed
3 celery ribs, chopped
1 small bunch parsley, chopped
1 Tbsp. fresh rosemary leaves, chopped
1 lb. French lentils
10 cups water
4 cups chicken broth
2 Tbsp. balsamic vinegar
Salt & pepper to taste

Heat olive oil in a large soup pot. Add onion & garlic, and sauté 7 minutes. Add celery, parsley and rosemary — sauté 5 minutes. Add lentils, water and broth.

Cover and bring to a boil. Reduce heat and simmer for 2 hours, stirring occasionally. Add vinegar, salt and pepper to taste.

Mix well — simmer 15 minutes and serve.

Suzy's Cream of Broccoli Soup

Low-fat... thanks to the evaporated skim milk ... and yet deliciously creamy.

• SERVES 6-8 •

2 Tbsp. olive oil
4 large cloves garlic, pressed
1 large onion, chopped
1 head broccoli, broken into florets
1 celery rib, coarsely chopped
2 carrots, coarsely chopped
2 medium all-purpose potatoes, peeled & chopped
¼ cup flour
4 cups chicken broth
4 cups water
1 tsp. dried parsley
salt & pepper to taste
1 12-oz. can evaporated skim milk

Heat olive oil in a large soup pot. Add garlic & onion. Sauté 5 minutes. Add broccoli, celery, carrots & potatoes. Sauté 5 minutes. Add flour & mix well. Add broth, water, parsley, and salt & pepper to taste. Cover & bring to a boil. Reduce heat & simmer for 1 hour. Purée vegetables and mix well. Add evaporated milk ~ mix again. Cover & simmer on low heat for 10 minutes. Serve.

White Bean and Porcini Mushroom Soup

The porcini mushrooms add a robust...almost meaty flavor. Serve with a crusty whole grain bread and a green salad.
NOTE THAT THE BEANS ARE SOAKED OVERNIGHT, SO PLAN ACCORDINGLY.

· SERVES 6-8 ·

1 lb. white navy beans
water to cover by 2" to soak overnight

8 cups water
2 oz. dried porcini mushrooms
1 cup hot water for soaking
3 Tbsp. olive oil
7 large cloves garlic, pressed
1 large onion, chopped
½ cup Marsala wine
1 Tbsp. balsamic vinegar
2 cups chicken broth
1 2-lb. can crushed tomatoes
2 Tbsp. fresh chopped thyme
1 Tbsp. fresh chopped rosemary
1 Tbsp. dried basil
1 Tbsp. dried parsley
salt & pepper to taste

Put beans in a large bowl — cover with water and set aside to soak overnight.

The next day, discard water and put beans into a large soup pot. Add 8 cups water. Cover and bring to a boil. Reduce heat and simmer while you place porcini mushrooms into a bowl and add water. Set aside to soak for 1 hour.

While the mushrooms are soaking and the beans are cooking, heat olive oil in a skillet. Add garlic and onion — sauté 7 minutes. Add wine and vinegar — sauté 5 minutes. Add skillet contents to pot of beans, along with chicken broth, tomatoes, herbs, and salt & pepper to taste. Cover and simmer.

After 1 hour of soaking, add mushrooms along with their soaking liquid to the pot.

Cover and continue cooking another 1½ hours, stirring occasionally.

After 1½ hours, mash beans slightly with a potato masher. Add more salt & pepper if needed and serve.

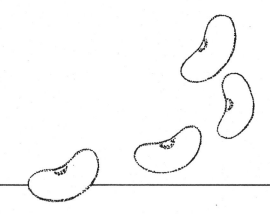

Miso Soup

Takes so little time to prepare, is very delicious and so-ooooo very good for you. I like it plain, but my children prefer it with a scoop or two of brown rice.

· SERVES 6-8 ·

1 cup brown rice
2 Tbsp. roasted sesame oil
1 bunch scallions, chopped
1 large clove garlic, pressed
2 Tbsp. freshly grated ginger
1 6" piece of Kombu seaweed, cut into small
                                              pieces
1 lb. firm tofu, cut into small cubes
4 large carrots, cut into thin rounds
2 quarts water
$\frac{2}{3}$-1 cup yellow or white miso

Cook rice as directed. While the rice is cooking, heat sesame oil in a large soup pot. Add scallions, garlic, ginger & Kombu — sauté 5 minutes. Add tofu, carrots and water. Cover & bring to a boil — reduce heat & simmer, covered, 30 minutes. After 30 minutes, ladle out 2 cups liquid from pot — mix with miso — return to pot and mix well. Heat for 5 minutes... do not boil, as it kills off the beneficial properties of the miso. Serve as is, or with rice added to each bowl.

Cream of Summer Squash Soup

If you've ever grown summer squash, I'm sure I don't need to tell you that you really have to stretch your imagination to come up with ideas for cooking the millions of squash harvested daily! This soup turned out great & my young son loved it. It was puréed, so he couldn't see all the healthy veggies lurking within.

· SERVES 6-8

2 Tbsp. butter
1 medium onion, chopped
2 carrots, cut into rounds
3 medium potatoes, chopped
2 medium yellow squash, chopped
2 cups chicken or vegetable broth
6 cups water
2 Tbsp. fresh thyme, chopped
¼ cup fresh parsley, chopped
salt to taste
½ cup Half & Half

Melt butter in a large soup pot with lid. Add onion & sauté 5 minutes. Add carrots, potatoes & squash – sauté 5 min. Add broth and water. Cover & bring to a boil. Reduce heat to low, and add thyme, parsley, & salt to taste. Simmer for 40 minutes, covered. Purée in a food processor or blender. Put puréed veggies back into pot & stir well. Add Half & Half. Stir. Cover & heat on low for 10 minutes. Serve.

Curried Black Bean Soup

A hearty dish, falling somewhere between a soup and a stew. Serve with warm corn bread.

· MAKES A BIG POT ·

2 cups dry black beans or 3 10-oz. cans of cooked black beans (if using dry beans, cover with water & soak overnight)

3 Tbsp. olive oil

1 onion, peeled & chopped

3 large cloves garlic, pressed

1 cup brown Basmati rice (rinse well)

2 carrots, chopped

2 celery ribs, chopped

1 yam, peeled & chopped

3 Tbsp. ground cumin

3 Tbsp. curry powder

1 Tbsp. ground fennel seed

1 Tbsp. ground coriander seed

juice of 1 orange

2 cups canned tomatoes

12 cups water

salt to taste

> **NOTE:** If using dry beans, soak overnight. Discard water the next day. Place beans in a large pot & cover with water. Cover & bring to a boil. Reduce heat & simmer on low heat for 2 hours. Forget all of this if using canned beans!

> **SERVING TIP:** A dollop of plain yogurt can be added to each bowl if desired.

Heat olive oil in a skillet, add onion & garlic — sauté 5 minutes. Add rice, carrots, celery, yam & spices. Sauté 5 minutes. Put skillet contents into a large soup pot with black beans. Add tomatoes, water & a little salt. Cover & bring to a boil. Reduce heat & simmer 1 hour. Add orange juice & more salt if needed. Cook ½ hour & serve.

Mexican Corn Chowder

very yummy !

· SERVES 8-12 ·

2 Tbsp. butter

1 medium onion chopped

3 large cloves garlic, pressed

1 dried Ancho pepper .... remove and discard seeds, break pepper into small pieces ... if you can't get an Ancho, then substitute with 3 Tbsp. Chili Powder

3 Tbsp. ground cumin

3 carrots, coarsely chopped

6 medium potatoes, coarsely chopped

2 lb. frozen corn kernels

4 cups chicken or vegetable broth

12 cups water

2 cups canned crushed tomatoes

2 Tbsp. fresh cilantro, chopped

salt

Melt butter in a large pot ~ add onion & garlic ~ sauté 5 minutes. Add Ancho pepper (or chili powder) & cumin. Mix well. Add carrots, potatoes, ½ of the corn (1 lb.), broth, water & tomatoes. Cover & bring to a boil. Reduce heat & simmer, covered, for 45 minutes. Remove from heat & purée vegetables. Return veggies to pot & mix well. Add remaining corn, cilantro & salt to taste. Simmer for 30 minutes and serve.

Sweet and Sour Borscht

My mother (one of the world's greatest cooks) used to make this wonderful Borscht with meat. Every time she served it, my father (one of the world's greatest food connoisseurs) would exclaim, "It takes just like a fine wine!" I wasn't certain that I could reproduce the same effect, especially without the meat. However, I must say that I was very pleased with the results. My mother's spirit must have been in the kitchen guiding me that day.

· MAKES A LARGE POT... FEEDS A CROWD ·

4 Tbsp. butter (a good & necessary substitute for the meat)
1 large Spanish onion, chopped
3 large cloves garlic, chopped
7 large beets, peeled & cut into bite-size pieces
6 large all-purpose potatoes, scrubbed & cut into bite-size pieces
1 small green cabbage, or ½ large cabbage, sliced
2 cups canned crushed tomatoes
12 cups water
1 Tbsp. salt
1 cup turbinado or white sugar
juice of 2 large lemons

SERVING TIP: SERVE ALONE OR WITH A DOLLOP OF SOUR CREAM IN THE MIDDLE OF EACH BOWL

Melt butter in a large soup pot. Add onion & garlic ⁓ sauté on low heat for 10 minutes. Add beets, potatoes & cabbage ⁓ sauté 3 minutes. Add tomatoes, water & salt. Cover & bring to a boil. Lower heat & simmer, covered, for 1 hour, stirring occasionally. Add sugar & lemon juice ⁓ mix well. Cover and simmer 20 minutes.

Cream of Potato Soup

Creamy smooth ~ tastes rich without actually being so.

• MAKES A GOOD-SIZE POTFUL •

3 Tbsp. butter
1 large onion, chopped
¼ cup fresh parsley, chopped
½ cup fresh dill, chopped
7 large all-purpose potatoes, scrubbed and
               coarsely chopped (leave skins on)
4 cups chicken or vegetable stock
8 cups water
salt & pepper to taste
1 cup Half & Half or whole milk

Melt butter in a large pot & add onions. Sauté
5 minutes. Add parsley, dill and potatoes.
Sauté 5 minutes. Add broth, water, a little
salt and pepper. Cover and bring to a boil.
Reduce heat to low and simmer, covered, for
40 minutes. Purée veggies. Mix the puréed
veggies back into the broth. Add Half & Half.
Taste to see if more salt and pepper is
needed.
Heat on low for 10 minutes. Serve garnished with
a little chopped leafy dill frond, or paprika.

Minestrone

A hearty soup! Serve with a green salad and a crusty bread, or a loaf of warm garlic bread. Sometimes I add a few cheese Tortellinis, which really transforms it into a meal unto itself.

· MAKES A LARGE POT... SERVES 6-10 ·

3 Tbsp. olive oil
1 large onion, chopped
4 large cloves garlic, pressed
¼ cup fresh parsley, chopped
¼ cup fresh basil, chopped
7 large Swiss Chard leaves, chopped
1 medium summer squash, chopped
2 large carrots, chopped
2 large Bliss potatoes, chopped
1 19-oz. can cannellini beans
1 19-oz. can red Kidney beans
2 cups chicken or vegetable broth
¼ cup dry white or red wine
5 fresh tomatoes, chopped, or 1 1-lb. can tomatoes
10 cups water
salt & pepper to taste
1 cup freshly grated Locatelli cheese

Heat olive oil in a large soup pot — add onion & garlic — sauté for 7 minutes. Add parsley, basil, Swiss chard,

squash, carrots and potatoes — sauté 5 minutes.
Add beans, broth, wine, tomatoes, water, and
some salt & pepper.
Cover pot and bring to a boil, then reduce heat &
simmer, covered, 1½ hours. Taste to see if more
salt is needed and serve.
Pass grated cheese around table, or sprinkle a
teaspoon or so on top of each bowl when serving.

Lentil Soup

You must serve this soup with a very crusty bread ~ I alone can dip a whole loaf into the soup at one sitting, granted after which I need to be helped from my seat by several family members!

· feeds the masses ·

¼ cup olive oil
1 large Spanish onion, chopped
7 large cloves garlic, pressed
2 Tbsp. fresh thyme, chopped
2 Tbsp. fresh rosemary, chopped
¼ cup fresh flat-leaf parsley, chopped
3 Tbsp. balsamic vinegar (a must)
7 large Swiss chard leaves, chopped
¼ lb. mushrooms, sliced
1 lb. brown lentils
4 cups chicken or vegetable broth
14 cups water
4 cups canned tomatoes
Salt & pepper to taste
1 cup freshly grated Parmesan or Romano
                              Cheese

Heat oil in a large soup pot ~ add onion, garlic, thyme, rosemary and parsley ~ sauté 10 minutes on a low heat. Add balsamic vinegar, Swiss chard, &

mushrooms — sauté 5 minutes. Add lentils, broth, water, tomatoes, salt and pepper. Mix well — Cover and bring to a boil. Reduce heat to low & cook, covered, 3 hours, stirring often.

Ladle soup into bowls — sprinkle a generous amount of grated cheese over top, and serve.

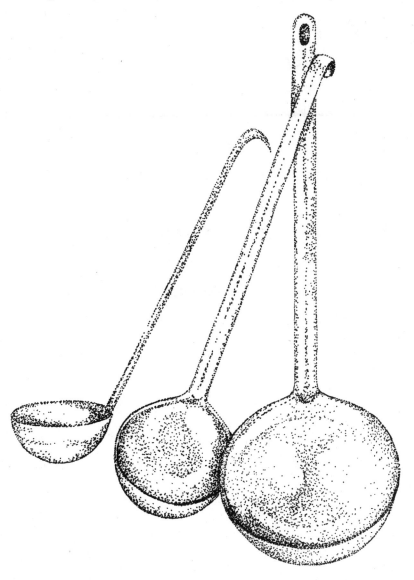

Curried Butternut Squash Soup

~ an interesting blending of flavors

· SERVES 6-8 ·

1 medium butternut squash ~ peeled, seeds
                                                   removed & cubed
2 medium apples ~ peeled, cored & quartered
7 cups of water
2 Tbsp. butter
1 small onion, chopped
2 large cloves garlic, pressed
2 Tbsp. fresh cilantro, chopped
2 carrots, chopped
1 celery rib, chopped
3 Tbsp. curry powder
2 Tbsp. ground cumin seed
$\frac{1}{2}$ cup raisins
2 cups chicken or vegetable broth
1 cup sour cream or yogurt
salt to taste

Place squash, apples and water in a large
soup pot. Cover and bring to a boil ~ reduce
heat and simmer as you melt butter in a
skillet. Add onion and garlic; sauté 5 minutes.

Add cilantro, carrots and celery — sauté 5 minutes. Add curry powder, cumin & raisins, and sauté 5 minutes. Add skillet contents to squash and apples. Add broth — cover & return to a boil. Reduce heat and simmer 1 hour.

Purée veggies however you like to do so — either in a food processor or blender. After they are puréed and back in the pot, mix well. Add sour cream or yogurt, and salt to taste. Mix well. Cover and heat on a low heat for 10 minutes or so. Do not boil.

Seafood Chowder

Special!

·MAKES A BIG POT·

3 Tbsp. butter
1 medium red onion, chopped
2 large cloves garlic, pressed
4 Tbsp. flour
¼ cup Pernod (licorice-flavored liqueur)
3 carrots, chopped
2 celery ribs, chopped
½ cup fresh parsley, chopped

¼ cup fresh thyme, chopped
2 cups canned tomatoes
10 cups water
1 lb. scrod, cut in pieces (check for bones)
1 lb. bay scallops
1 lb. fresh clams, chopped
salt & pepper to taste
1 cup Half & Half

Melt butter in a large soup pot ⌣ add onion & garlic. Sauté 5 minutes. Add flour & mix well to form a roux. Add Pernod & mix well. Add carrots, celery, parsley, thyme, tomatoes and water. Cover and bring to a boil. Reduce heat to low and simmer 40 minutes. Add scrod, scallops, clams, and some salt & pepper. Simmer, uncovered, for 15 minutes. Add Half & Half, then taste to see if it needs more salt & pepper. Heat on a low heat for 10 minutes. Do not boil ⌣ serve.

Vegetable Broth

For strict vegetarians a vegetable broth is a good substitute for chicken broth.

· MAKES APPROXIMATELY 2 QUARTS ·

4 carrots, scrubbed & coarsely chopped
2 onions, peeled & quartered
4 celery ribs, coarsely chopped
3 garlic cloves, peeled & left whole
1 large all-purpose potato, scrubbed & coarsely chopped
2 parsnips, peeled & coarsely chopped
1 bunch parsley
2 bay leaves
12 cups water
salt & pepper to taste

Place all of the above ingredients in a large stock pot. Cover and bring to a boil. Reduce heat and simmer for 1 hour. Strain the liquid stock through a sieve and discard vegetables.

Allow the broth to cool, then refrigerate or freeze in 1 to 2 cup containers.

    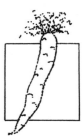

Fish Stock

When making fish stews, soups & chowders, often the fish is added at the end to prevent overcooking. Consequently the dish may not have much of a fish flavor. A fish stock can add the extra kick needed. Ask your fish market to give you a few fish heads and you'll be in business! Also if the recipe calls for shrimp or lobster, save the shells & add to stock.

· MAKES APPROXIMATELY 1 QUART ·

3 or 4 fish heads
shells from shrimp or lobster
1 large onion, peeled & cut in half
2 carrots, coarsely chopped
2 celery ribs, coarsely chopped
1 small bunch parsley
a few sprigs of thyme and/or tarragon
2 bay leaves
10 cups water

Place all of the above ingredients into a large stock pot. Cover and bring to a boil. Reduce heat and simmer for ½ hour. Discard heads, shells and vegetables. Strain stock through a mesh strainer. Use stock or allow to cool, then refrigerate, or freeze in 1 to 2 cup containers.

Chicken Stock

Chicken stock is good to have on hand. Of course, one can buy canned stock, but I personally don't like using stock that is not made from organically raised chickens. Therefore I make my own and freeze it in small containers to use when needed.

· MAKES APPROXIMATELY 2 QUARTS ·

1 3-4 lb. chicken, cut up
12 cups water
1 large onion, peeled & left whole
1 small bunch parsley
3 carrots, scrubbed & coarsely chopped
3 celery ribs, coarsely chopped
2 parsnips, peeled & coarsely chopped
1 yam, peeled & cut in half
salt to taste

Rinse chicken and cut off excess fat. Place all of the above ingredients into a large stock pot. Cover and bring to a boil. Skim off any foam from top & discard. Reduce heat & simmer 1 hour.
Remove chicken from pot and save for chicken salad, chicken sandwiches, etc. Remove all other veggies from pot. Strain the stock through a sieve. Allow stock to cool, then refrigerate or freeze in small 1 to 2 cup containers.

NOTE: After stock has been chilled, the fat will come to the top and solidify – remove & discard the excess fat before using.

Pasta & a Risotto

Patti's Fettuccine with Roasted Pepper & Sun-Dried Tomato Sauce

· SERVES 4 ·

4 large red bell peppers – cored, seeded & cut into quarters
½ cup sun-dried tomatoes (dry pack)
2 cups boiling water
1 lb. fettuccine pasta
2 Tbsp. butter
¾ cup Half & Half
¼ cup freshly grated Parmesan cheese
salt & pepper

Place pepper pieces onto a cookie sheet. Put in the oven about 4" from top broiler flame. Broil till skins are charred black. Remove from oven, place in a brown paper bag, close bag up tightly & let sit to cool 20 minutes. Meanwhile, place sun-dried tomatoes into a bowl – add boiling water & let soak 20 minutes. Begin to cook pasta as directed. Remove peppers from bag & slip charred skins off. Place peppers into a food processor or blender. Drain water from sun-dried tomatoes & add to peppers. Process until smooth. Set aside while melting butter in a pot on low heat. Add pepper & sun-dried mixture – stir on a low heat. Gradually add Half & Half, cheese, and salt & pepper to taste. Mix well and cook on low heat 3 minutes. Drain pasta & place into a large pasta bowl. Add sauce... mix and serve.

Angel Hair Pasta with Spicy Marinara Sauce

· SERVES 6-8 ·

4 Tbsp. olive oil
1 medium yellow onion, chopped
10 large cloves garlic, pressed
¼ cup dry white wine
2 2-lb. cans whole peeled Italian tomatoes,
  "smush" with hands

2 Tbsp. chopped fresh basil
1 Tbsp. chopped fresh oregano
½-1 tsp. hot red pepper flakes
1 Tbsp. raw sugar
salt to taste
2 lbs. angel hair pasta
1 cup freshly grated Parmesan or Romano cheese

Heat oil in a large pot ~ add onion & garlic ~ sauté for
10 minutes. Add wine, tomatoes, herbs, hot pepper, sugar,
and salt to taste. Mix well & cook, uncovered, for one
hour, stirring often.
After the sauce has been cooking for ½ hour, begin
cooking pasta as directed. Drain pasta & return to pot.
Mix with half of the sauce ~ mix well.
Transfer pasta to a large pasta bowl & ladle remaining
sauce over top. Serve. Pass cheese around the table.

Pasta à la Fungi

~ just another quick way to adorn our beloved pasta!

. SERVES 4 .

1 lb. linguini or other pasta of choice
4 Tbsp. olive oil
10 large cloves garlic, pressed
½ lb. fresh shiitake mushrooms, sliced
1 lb. Portobello mushrooms, sliced
1 lb. white mushrooms, sliced
4 cups canned tomatoes
¼ cup dry white wine
3 Tbsp. capers
salt & pepper to taste
1 tsp. dried parsley
1 tsp. dried basil
1 cup freshly grated Romano or Parmesan cheese

Begin to cook pasta as directed. Meanwhile, heat olive oil in a large skillet — add garlic and mushrooms — sauté 7 minutes. Add remaining ingredients except for the cheese. Cover and simmer on a medium heat for 20 minutes. Drain pasta and put back into pot. Add contents from skillet, and mix well. Sprinkle about ½ cup cheese over top & toss again. Put pasta in a large bowl & serve. Pass extra cheese around the table.

Pesto Genovese

The addition of potatoes, either broiled or roasted, transforms Pesto into Pesto Genovese — though this may sound strange, I assure you it's amazing. Follow the recipe for Garlic Roasted Potatoes — however, cut the recipe in half unless you plan on feeding an army.

· SERVES 6-8 ·

Garlic Roasted Potatoes (see pg. 147)
2 lbs. ziti or penne pasta
PESTO:
1 large bunch fresh basil leaves, coarsely chopped
1 medium bunch fresh parsley, coarsely chopped
4 Tbsp. olive oil
3 large cloves garlic, peeled & coarsely chopped
1 fresh ripe tomato (optional)
¼ lb. fresh Romano cheese, cut into slivers
1 cup pine nuts or walnuts

Start roasting potatoes 1½ hours before you plan on serving dinner. During the last ½ hour that the potatoes are roasting, put up the water for pasta. Meanwhile, make pesto by placing all the pesto ingredients into a food processor or blender & whirl till smooth. Set aside till pasta is cooked. Drain pasta & return to pot. Add pesto paste & mix well. Add roasted potatoes & mix well. Transfer to a large pasta bowl & serve.

Wonderful Quick Linguini

Maybe we should have called this..."Linguini à la Jar"... as it's a jar of this, and a jar of that! But, whatever... it works!!

· SERVES 4 ·

1 lb. linguini
¼ cup olive oil
4 large cloves garlic, pressed
1 cup black pitted olives, cut in half
1 4-oz. jar roasted red peppers, cut in bite-size pieces
1 4-oz. jar marinated artichoke hearts, cut in bite-size pieces
4 sun-dried tomatoes, chopped - packed in oil
¼ lb. freshly grated Parmesan or Romano cheese
salt to taste
a few shakes of hot pepper flakes

Begin cooking pasta as directed. In the meantime, pour olive oil into a large skillet ~heat~ add garlic and sauté 3 minutes. Then add olives, roasted peppers, artichoke hearts & sun-dried tomatoes. Sauté 5 minutes. Drain pasta, return to pot, and add contents of skillet. Add cheese, salt & a few hot pepper flakes.

Toss well and serve.

Chilled Sesame Soba Noodles

If you haven't tried soba noodles, you are in for a treat. Buy soba with whole wheat flour added... 100% buckwheat soba is a bit intense for our liking.

• SERVES 4 •

    2 Tbsp. sesame seeds
    1 lb. soba noodles
    3 Tbsp. roasted sesame oil
    3 Tbsp. tamari
    1 Tbsp. freshly grated ginger

Roast sesame seeds by placing them into a dry skillet... heat on a medium flame for a few minutes until seeds are golden (be careful, as they cook quickly). Remove seeds from pan and set aside.

Cook noodles as directed on package — do not overcook! Drain in a colander and run cold water over noodles for a few minutes to chill. Drain well, return to pot, add remaining ingredients, sprinkle with roasted seeds. Refrigerate 1 hour or more before serving.

Pasta Foresta

Bow tie pasta lightly coated with a creamy mush‑room sauce.

· SERVES 4 ·

1 lb. bow tie pasta (farfalle)
7 sun-dried tomatoes (packed in oil), cut into strips
3 Tbsp. olive oil
7 large cloves garlic, pressed
2 shallots, chopped
1 lb. fresh mushrooms, sliced
1 tsp. dried oregano
⅛ cup dry white wine
salt & pepper
½ cup half & half
1 cup freshly grated Parmesan cheese

Start water for pasta and cook as directed. Meanwhile, place sun-dried tomatoes, oil, garlic & shallots into a large skillet ⌐ sauté 5 minutes. Add mushrooms & sauté 7 minutes. Add oregano, wine, salt & pepper to taste. Sauté on medium heat for 7 minutes. Add half & half. Mix well. Cook on low heat for 5 minutes. Drain pasta & put back in pot. Add skillet contents & grated cheese. Toss well and serve.

Fettuccine Alfredo

Traditionally, Fettuccine Alfredo has been made with lots of butter and heavy cream — a real artery blocker! But life without it really isn't an option ... so, somehow we learn to compromise. I have found that you can substitute olive oil for all or ½ of the butter, and Half & Half for the heavy cream. It is, however, very important to use a good fresh grating cheese to compensate for the changes. I like to combine ½ Romano with ½ Parmesan, but all of one or the other will do.

· SERVES 3-4 ·

1 lb. Fettuccine pasta
¼ cup olive oil (or 2 Tbsp. butter & 2 Tbsp. olive oil)
1 clove garlic, pressed
2 Tbsp. fresh parsley, chopped (or 1 Tbsp. dried)
1 cup Half & Half
½ cup freshly grated Romano cheese
½ cup freshly grated Parmesan cheese
salt & pepper to taste

Begin cooking pasta as directed. The sauce for this takes 10 minutes to make, so it will be ready by the time the pasta is done.

Heat oil in a small pot — add garlic. After about one minute, add parsley and Half & Half. Cook on a low heat until hot, stirring often — do not boil. Drain pasta and put back in pot. Pour sauce over top — add cheese, salt & lots of freshly ground pepper. Toss well & serve immediately.

NOTE: Sometimes I squeeze a lemon over top & toss right before serving for a little change of pace.

Pasta Primavera

— it's a spring thing!

· SERVES 4 ·

1 lb. linguine
¼ cup olive oil
10 cloves garlic, pressed
1 lb. asparagus, chopped
½ lb. snow peas or sugar snap peas — remove
stems
salt & pepper
juice of 1 lemon
2 Tbsp. capers
3 sun-dried tomatoes packed in oil, chopped
12 pitted black olives, halved
1 lb. fresh spinach, rinsed & chopped
¼ lb. freshly grated Romano cheese

Begin cooking pasta as directed. Meanwhile, heat olive
oil in a large skillet and add garlic — sauté 3 minutes.
Add asparagus — sauté 7 minutes. Add snow peas, salt &
pepper, lemon juice, capers, sun-dried tomatoes and
olives — sauté 5 minutes. Remove from heat — add spinach and toss well.
Drain pasta and put back into pot. Add skillet contents.
Mix well. Add cheese and toss again. Transfer to a
large pasta bowl and serve.

Ziti with a Spicy Puttanesca Sauce

Anchovies, Kalamata olives and capers give this spicy tomato sauce a delightful piquant flavor.

· SERVES 6-8 ·

¼ cup olive oil
1 large Spanish onion, chopped
1 large whole head garlic, peeled & minced
3 anchovies, chopped (or a 3" squirt anchovy paste)
¼ cup fresh parsley, chopped
½ cup fresh arugula, chopped (optional)
½ tsp. hot red pepper flakes
½ cup dry white wine
2 2-lb. cans tomatoes
4 Tbsp. capers
16 Kalamata olives, pitted & cut into pieces
1 tsp. salt (or to taste)
1 tsp. raw sugar or honey
1 cup freshly grated Parmesan or Romano cheese
2 lbs. ziti pasta

Heat oil in a large heavy-bottom sauce pot. Add onion and garlic – sauté on a medium heat for 10 minutes. Add anchovies, parsley, arugula, hot pepper flakes and wine. Sauté

5 minutes. Add tomatoes, capers, olives, salt, and sugar. Cook, uncovered, on a low heat for 1 hour.

Prepare pasta as directed. Drain, put into a large pasta bowl, and ladle half of the sauce over pasta.

Put the extra sauce into another bowl, and pass around the table, along with the grated cheese.

→ a winner!

Pasta Misto

Another extraordinary pasta experience...!

· SERVES 6 ·

1½ lbs. rigatoni pasta
¼ cup olive oil
7 large garlic cloves, pressed
2 shallots, chopped
7 sun-dried tomatoes (packed in oil), cut into strips
1 head radicchio, chopped
1 Belgian endive, chopped
1 fennel bulb, chopped
¼ lb. fresh shiitake mushrooms, sliced
¼ cup fresh chopped parsley
¼ cup dry white wine
2 Tbsp. balsamic vinegar
salt & pepper to taste
¼ lb. freshly grated Parmesan or Romano cheese

Cook pasta as directed. Meanwhile heat oil in a large skillet ~ add garlic & shallots. Sauté 5 minutes. Add sun-dried tomatoes, radicchio, endive, fennel, shiitake mushrooms & parsley ~ sauté for 7 minutes. Add wine, vinegar, and salt & pepper to taste. Sauté 5 minutes. Drain pasta, put back into pot and add skillet contents. Toss & transfer to a large pasta bowl. Serve. Pass the cheese around the table.

Shiitake Mushroom and Sun-Dried Tomato Risotto

~Delizioso!

· SERVES 4-6 ·

3 Tbsp. olive oil
1 large clove garlic, pressed
3 large shallots, chopped
10 sun-dried tomatoes (packed in oil) ~ drained and sliced

4 oz. shiitake mushrooms
2 cups Arborio rice
3 cups chicken or vegetable broth
3 cups water
1 cup dry white wine
½ cup freshly grated Parmesan cheese
salt & pepper

Heat olive oil in a heavy pot ~ add garlic & shallots ~ sauté 5 minutes. Add sun-dried tomatoes & mushrooms. Sauté 5 minutes. Add rice & stir well to coat. Meanwhile, heat broth, water & wine in another pot. Add ½ cup liquid to the rice. Cook uncovered on a very low heat till most of the liquid is absorbed, stirring constantly to prevent sticking. Keep repeating the above process until all liquid is used (this takes about ½ hour). Add cheese and a little salt and pepper. Stir well & serve immediately.

<u>Vegetarian Meatballs & Spaghetti</u>

These meatballs are made with an interesting product — T.V.P.,
or Texturized Vegetable Protein. Don't ask me to explain it,
but it works... it's natural... no cholesterol... and it makes
a great vegetarian meatball. Our dear, although rarely seen,
friend Jay DiMarco, who was a strict vegetarian at the time,
was so delighted, as he thought he'd never enjoy a good meatball again...!

· SERVES 6-8 ·

<u>SAUCE</u>

3 Tbsp. olive oil
7 large cloves garlic, pressed
1 small onion
2 Tbsp. freshly chopped parsley
2 Tbsp. fresh basil or oregano, chopped
¼ cup dry white or red wine
salt to taste
a few shakes of hot pepper flakes (optional)
2 2-lb. cans crushed plum tomatoes
....
2 lbs. spaghetti pasta
1 cup freshly grated Parmesan cheese

<u>To make sauce</u> ~ heat oil in a large pot ~ add garlic,
onion and herbs. Sauté 10 minutes. Add wine, salt,
a few shakes of hot pepper flakes, and tomatoes. Cook
uncovered on a low heat, stirring often.

... while the sauce is cooking, make the meatballs ⟶

MEATBALLS

2 cups dry T.V.P. (sold at natural food stores)
2 cups warm water
2 eggs, beaten
5 large cloves garlic, pressed
1 small onion, finely chopped
2 Tbsp. fresh parsley, chopped
1 cup freshly grated Parmesan cheese
2 cups grated mozzarella cheese
1 + cup seasoned bread crumbs
salt to taste

olive oil for frying

To make meatballs — place the T.V.P. into a large bowl.
Add water & let sit for 20 minutes. Then pour the T.V.P.
into a colander to drain off excess water. Put back into bowl & add remaining ingredients except for the oil.
Form into balls (add more bread crumbs if balls don't
hold together). Heat oil in a large skillet & add balls
(do not overcrowd). Cook on medium heat 5 minutes.
Keep flipping balls to brown on all sides (very important, so be patient). Remove from pan & repeat with
the remaining balls, then carefully drop into sauce.
Cover & cook on low for 1 hour. Do not stir whilst they
are cooking, as you may mush them.

Cook pasta as directed & drain. Put into a bowl & spoon
sauce & balls over top. Serve. Place grated cheese on table.

Ziti with Wild Mushrooms & Fennel

There are so many different varieties of mushrooms on the market ~ both domestic & wild. Fennel is a wonderful vegetable so often overlooked.

· SERVES 4 ·

1 lb. ziti
¼ cup olive oil
1 small onion, chopped
7 large cloves garlic, pressed
1 bunch fresh parsley, chopped
12 fresh shiitake mushrooms, sliced
6 oz. crimini or white mushrooms, sliced
4 oz. oyster mushrooms, sliced
1 small head fennel (anise), sliced
¼ cup pine nuts
6 sun-dried tomatoes, chopped (packed in oil)
12 pitted black olives, cut in half
a few shakes of hot pepper flakes
¼ cup dry white or red wine
             (whichever you have on hand)
salt to taste
½ cup freshly grated Parmesan cheese

Start water for pasta. In a large skillet, heat oil ~ add onion and garlic. Sauté 5 minutes.

Add parsley, all mushrooms and fennel. Sauté 5 minutes. Add pine nuts, sun-dried tomatoes, olives, hot pepper flakes, wine and salt. Cook uncovered for 10 minutes, stirring often. While it's cooking, your pasta should also be cooking. Drain pasta and put back into pot. Add skillet contents to pasta and toss well. Add grated cheese – toss again and serve.

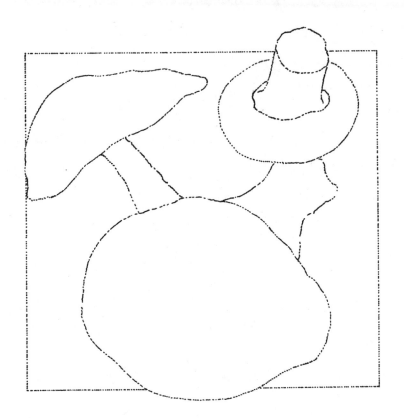

Mushroom Ragoût over Farfalle

A ragoût is a flavorful thick stew often made with fish, chicken or vegetables.....this one is loaded with 3 different kinds of mushrooms. I like to serve it over bow tie pasta, but feel free to serve it alongside rice or by itself, accompanying grilled fish or chicken. Note that the dried porcini mushrooms need an hour to soak, so plan accordingly.

· SERVES 4 ·

delicious!

1 oz. dried porcini mushrooms
1 cup boiling water
1 lb. farfalle pasta (bow ties)
¼ cup olive oil
7 large cloves garlic, pressed
3 shallots, chopped
7 sun-dried tomatoes (packed in oil), drained and cut into strips
¼ lb. fresh shiitake mushrooms, sliced
1 lb. fresh white mushrooms, sliced
½ cup sherry
1 Tbsp. dried parsley flakes
2 Tbsp. fresh thyme, chopped
1 Tbsp. fresh marjoram, chopped
salt & pepper
1 cup half & half
1 cup freshly grated Parmesan cheese

One hour before beginning dinner, place porcini mushrooms into a bowl ~ pour boiling water over top and let sit.

One hour later... drain porcini mushrooms & save soaking liquid... set aside.

Begin cooking pasta as directed.

Meanwhile ~ heat oil in a large skillet. Add garlic and shallots, and sauté 5 minutes. Add sun-dried tomatoes and the porcini, shiitake & white mushrooms (do not add soaking liquid) ~ sauté 5 minutes. Add sherry, herbs, and salt & pepper to taste, plus ½ cup of the soaking liquid (ditch the rest). Cover and simmer 20 minutes.

While ragoût is simmering, the pasta should be cooking (timing is everything... they say).

Add half & half to mushrooms ~ mix well and simmer, uncovered, for 5 minutes. Drain the pasta and put into a large pasta bowl. Add skillet contents and mix well. Sprinkle with a little cheese and serve.

Place the remaining cheese on the table.

Bows, Cauliflower and Anchovies

This is my version of a classic Italian recipe. The ingredients may sound weird if not downright ghastly ... but, trust me, they work.

· SERVES 4-6 ·

1 lb. bow pasta (farfalle)
½ cup pine nuts
½ cup bread crumbs
1 large head cauliflower, broken into florets
Water
¼ cup olive oil
3 anchovies, chopped (or a good 5" squirt of anchovy paste)

2 large cloves garlic, pressed
¼ tsp. hot red pepper flakes
¼ cup raisins
¼ cup Marsala wine
juice of 1 lemon
½ cup freshly grated Romano cheese

Put up water for pasta as directed on package. Place pine nuts into a dry skillet and toast on a low heat for 5 minutes, stirring to prevent burning — set aside.

Place bread crumbs in same skillet and toast them for 3 minutes. Add to pine nuts and set aside.

Place cauliflower florets into a pot & cover with about an inch of water. Cover and steam for 5 minutes. Drain in colander.

Most likely the water for the pasta has boiled... Cook pasta as directed.

Meanwhile, heat olive oil in a large skillet ~ add anchovies, garlic, hot pepper flakes, raisins and steamed cauliflower. Cook on a medium heat for 5 minutes. Add wine and lemon, and cook 5 minutes.

Drain pasta in colander and put back into pot. Add skillet contents, pine nuts, bread crumbs and grated cheese.

Toss well and serve.

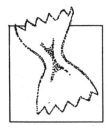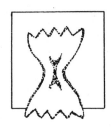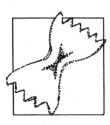

Ratatouille Over Rigatoni

...for lack of a better name!

· SERVES 6-10 ·

3 Tbsp. olive oil
1 onion, chopped
8 large cloves garlic, pressed
1 eggplant, peeled & cubed
2 zucchini, chopped
1 red bell pepper, chopped
½ cup fresh basil, chopped
2 quarts canned tomatoes
3 Tbsp. capers
hot red pepper flakes to taste
1 Tbsp. honey
salt to taste
2 lbs. rigatoni pasta
1 cup freshly grated Parmesan or Romano cheese

Heat oil in a large pot ~ add onion & garlic ~ sauté 5 minutes. Add eggplant, zucchini & pepper ~ sauté 10 minutes. Add basil, tomatoes, capers, some red pepper flakes, honey & salt to taste. Cover & simmer for ½ hour. While the sauce is simmering, cook pasta as directed. Drain cooked pasta in a colander. Serve in a large pasta bowl ~ add sauce & mix well. Sprinkle with cheese.

Tofu & Seitan

Tofu Sandwich Spread

This is a simple, tasty high-protein spread that is great on bread or rice cakes. Top it off with some fresh sprouts, sliced tomatoes and onion.

· SERVES 6-8 ·

2 lbs. fresh tofu
½ cup tahini
juice of 1 lemon
2 Tbsp. tamari
1 large clove garlic, pressed

Crumble tofu in a bowl with hands. Add remaining ingredients. Mash well with a potato masher.

Serve chilled or at room temperature.

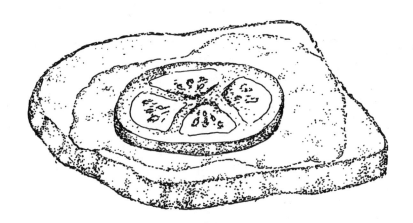

Great-Tasting Tofu

This is our favorite tofu recipe — haven't met a person yet who didn't love it... even die-hard tofu haters! There are two ways to make this tofu... for years I have always pan fried it & then baked it, but I have also eliminated the frying and just baked it. My husband likes it baked, but the rest of the family likes it fried a little first. You can use little oil to fry it — the idea is to get it slightly browned, as most of the cooking is done in the oven.

· SERVES 4 ·

2 lbs. firm tofu, cut into ¼" slices
¼ cup tamari
1 cup nutritional yeast
Canola oil

Preheat oven to 350°. Place tofu pieces onto a dish. Put tamari in one bowl and yeast in another bowl. Dip a piece of tofu into the tamari, then dip into yeast, and coat well. Set aside. Do this with all the tofu.

Cover the bottom of a skillet with oil & heat. Place as many pieces of tofu as possible into pan. Brown for 5 minutes on medium heat. Flip & brown the other side. Transfer to a large baking dish — repeat with remaining tofu. Bake tofu uncovered for 40 minutes. If you don't wish to fry the tofu first, place breaded tofu into an oiled baking pan and bake at 350° for 50 minutes.

Sheryl's Versatile Tofu Sandwiches

Sheryl makes these sandwiches whenever she's at a loss as to what to prepare for dinner... which is quite often! Serve on a whole grain bun with mayo, tomato, lettuce, onion, sprouts... the works!

• SERVES 3 to 4 •

1 lb. extra-firm tofu, cut into 12 thin slices
1 large clove garlic, pressed
½ cup tamari
peanut oil

Prepare tofu slices & set aside.

Put garlic and tamari into a bowl — dip tofu slices into tamari, and set aside.

Heat a little oil in a large skillet — place as many slices of tofu into skillet as possible. Cook on a medium heat until brown — flip tofu and brown on other side.

Place two or three slices of tofu onto each bun and do your thing.

Tofu, Soba and Veggies

Healthy and tasty. Soba is a Japanese buckwheat pasta that is very delicious and nutritious.

• SERVES 3-4 •

¼ cup sesame seeds

----

4 Tbsp. peanut oil
1 lb. firm tofu, cut into bite-size cubes
    (pat dry to remove all the moisture)
3 large cloves garlic
2 Tbsp. tamari

----

16 oz. soba noodles

----

2 Tbsp. safflower oil
3 large cloves garlic, pressed
1 bunch scallions, chopped
1 head broccoli, cut into florets
1 red bell pepper, sliced
½ lb. fresh shiitake mushrooms
2 celery ribs, coarsely chopped
2 carrots, coarsely chopped
¼ cup sherry
3 Tbsp. tamari (or to taste)

Place sesame seeds into a large skillet. Roast on a medium heat till golden (this takes only a few minutes, so be attentive), stirring often with a wooden spoon. Remove from heat and set aside.

In a wok or large skillet heat 4 Tbsp. peanut oil. Add 3 cloves garlic and the tofu cubes. Stir-fry over a medium/high heat until tofu is brown and crispy. Add 2 Tbsp. tamari and mix well. Remove tofu from wok & set aside.

Put up water for the soba. Cook as directed on package.

Meanwhile, in the same wok or skillet in which you cooked the tofu, heat 2 Tbsp. safflower oil — add the remaining 3 cloves of garlic, the scallions, broccoli, pepper, mushrooms, celery and carrots. Stir-fry on a medium/high heat about 7 minutes. Add tofu and stir-fry 5 minutes. Add sherry & tamari.

Drain soba noodles, add to wok and mix with the tofu and veggies.

Sprinkle seeds over top and serve.

Tofu Cacciatore

This recipe is a winner, if I must say so myself. It's basically the same as Chicken Cacciatore, but the tofu replaces the chicken. Serve over pasta, rice, cous-cous or polenta.

· SERVES 4-6 ·

2 lbs. firm tofu, cut into bite-size pieces
juice of 1 lemon
1 cup flour
salt & pepper to taste
4 Tbsp. olive oil

2 Tbsp. olive oil
1 medium onion, chopped
7 large cloves garlic, pressed
1 large red bell pepper, cut into bite-size pieces
1 lb. fresh mushrooms, halved
¼ cup dry white or red wine
1 2-lb. can tomatoes, chopped
1 Tbsp. dried basil
1 Tbsp. dried parsley
salt & pepper to taste
1 cup freshly grated Romano cheese

Place tofu cubes in a bowl ~ squeeze lemon over top. Put flour in another bowl. Add salt and pepper. Mix well. Put several pieces of to-fu into the flour to coat. Remove from bowl. Continue coating all the tofu cubes. Set aside.

Heat 2 Tbsp. oil in a large skillet. When hot, add enough tofu to cover bottom, but do not crowd. Cook on medium heat till bottom side is browned ~ flip over and brown other side. Continue flipping until all sides are nice and brown. Remove from pan. Repeat with rest of oil and tofu. Remove from pan and set aside.

In the same skillet, heat 2 Tbsp. olive oil ~ add onion and garlic ~ sauté 5 minutes. Add red pepper, and sauté another 5 minutes. Add mushrooms, wine, tomatoes, herbs, and a little salt & pepper. Cover & simmer on a low heat for ½ hour.

Add tofu cubes, cover and cook on low heat for 20 minutes.

Serve and sprinkle with a little grated cheese.

Tofitas

Inspired by the ever-popular Chicken Fajitas for the strict vegetarians in my family — very tasty.

· SERVES 4 to 6 ·

2 lbs. firm tofu, cut into long thin strips
juice of 1 lemon or lime
3 Tbsp. olive oil
1 Tbsp. cumin powder
1 Tbsp. chili powder
2 Tbsp. tamari

2 Tbsp. olive oil
2 large onions, sliced
3 large cloves garlic, pressed
2 red bell peppers, sliced
1 Tbsp. cumin powder
1 Tbsp. chili powder
salt to taste

12 6-inch flour tortillas, warmed
2 cups grated cheddar cheese
2 cups mild or hot salsa
1 avocado, peeled & cut into thin strips

Place tofu strips into a large bowl — add lemon, olive oil, cumin powder, chili powder & tamari. Stir gently to avoid breaking up the tofu. Place the tofu on a broiling pan and put in oven about 4 to 6" from top broiler flame. Broil 8 minutes on one side — then turn over and broil another 8 minutes.

While the tofu is broiling, heat 2 Tbsp. olive oil in a skillet — add onion and garlic, and sauté for 5 minutes. Add peppers, cumin, chili and salt to taste. Sauté 5 minutes. Cover and cook on a low heat for 10 minutes, stirring often.

Now the tofu and peppers should be ready. Place a warm tortilla on a dish — put a strip of tofu in the center... add a little of the peppers and onions, a sprinkle of cheese, a couple spoonfuls of salsa, and a strip of avocado. Roll up the tortilla and enjoy.

 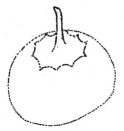 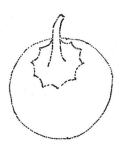

Thai-Style Seitan with Shiitake Mushrooms & Snow Peas

— delectable!

· SERVES 4-6 ·

2 cups of either brown basmati rice, white basmati rice or white jasmine rice

3½ cups water (brown rice requires 4 cups whereas the white rices require 3½ cups)

3 Tbsp. canola or safflower oil

6 large cloves garlic, pressed

1 bunch scallions, chopped

1 red bell pepper, sliced into thin strips

3 Tbsp. freshly grated ginger

2 lbs. seitan — cut into bite-size pieces

½ lb. shiitake mushrooms, sliced

1 Tbsp. hot chili paste or ½ tsp. hot red pepper flakes

1 Tbsp. fish sauce or tamari

1 cup hoison sauce

2 Tbsp. sherry

2 Tbsp. palm sugar or honey

¼ cup water

½ cup freshly chopped cilantro

½ lb. fresh snow peas

Cook rice as directed. While the rice is cooking, heat oil in a wok or large skillet – add garlic, whites of the scallions, bell pepper & ginger. Stir-fry for 5 minutes. Add seitan, shiitake mushrooms, hot chili paste, fish sauce, hiosin sauce, sherry, palm sugar & water. Stir-fry 7 minutes. Add cilantro, snow peas, and the remaining scallion greens. Stir-fry 7 minutes. Serve over rice.

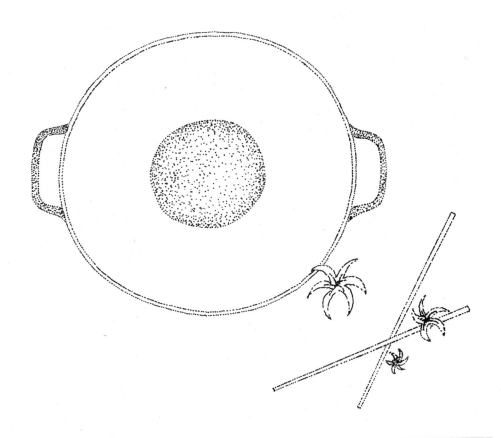

Sesame Baked Tofu

Serve with baked sweet potatoes, Kale and a salad.

· SERVES 4 ·

2 lbs. firm tofu, cut into quarters
1 Tbsp. roasted sesame oil
1 Tbsp. freshly grated ginger
$\frac{1}{8}$ cup tamari
$\frac{1}{8}$ cup water
$\frac{1}{4}$ cup sesame seeds

Preheat oven to 350°.

Place tofu pieces into a lightly oiled baking pan. Mix all the remaining ingredients together (except for the sesame seeds) in a bowl, and pour evenly over tofu.

Sprinkle sesame seeds over top and bake uncovered for 45 minutes at 350°.

Annie Lyn's Seitan for Aura

Great served with buttered noodles, salad & garlic bread.

· SERVES 2 ·

2 Tbsp. olive oil
1 small onion, chopped
2 large cloves garlic, pressed
2 carrots, sliced into rounds
2 celery ribs, coarsely chopped
8 oz. seitan, cut into bite-size pieces

½ lb. mushrooms
¼ cup dry white wine
salt
Cayenne pepper to taste
2 Tbsp. flour

Heat oil in a large cast iron skillet. Add onion and garlic — sauté 5 minutes. Add carrots and celery — sauté 7 minutes. Add seitan — sauté 5 minutes. Add mushrooms & sauté 5 minutes. Add wine, salt, and cayenne pepper to taste. Sauté 5 minutes and serve.

Seitan Stew

My children love this hearty stew... serve with a good crusty bread, as the sauce is perfect for dipping. It truly resembles a beef stew, as seitan's texture is so similar to tender beef. Try it... it's sure to make converts out of you.

· SERVES 4 ·

3 Tbsp. olive oil
1 onion, chopped
5 cloves garlic, pressed
3 stalks celery (leaves & all), coarsely chopped
3 large carrots, sliced into rounds
½ cup fresh chopped parsley
sprig of fresh thyme, chopped (optional)
8 medium Red Bliss potatoes, cut into quarters
　　　　(leave the skins on — scrub & rinse)
1 lb. seitan, cut into bite-size pieces
2 heaping Tbsp. flour
2 fresh tomatoes, chopped (optional)
5 cups water
¼ cup dry red wine, white wine, or sherry
tamari to taste

In a large heavy-bottom pot with lid, heat oil. Add onion & garlic — sauté 1 min. Add celery, carrots, parsley, thyme, potatoes & seitan — sauté 5 min. Add flour & mix well. Add remaining ingredients. Cover & simmer 1½ hours, stirring occasionally. Ladle into bowls and serve.

Main Course Vegetable Dishes

Indian Eggplant & Tomatoes

This is a mild, comforting Indian dish. I like to serve it with another more intense dish, such as a Spicy Curry together with Brown Basmati Rice & a Cucumber Raita.

· SERVES 4-6 ·

3 Tbsp. safflower oil
3 large cloves garlic, pressed
1 Tbsp. freshly grated ginger
3 Tbsp. ground cumin seed
1 Tbsp. ground coriander seed
1 Tbsp. ground fennel seed
2 large eggplants, peeled & cubed
4 large ripe tomatoes (or 2 cups canned)
salt to taste

Heat oil in a large skillet ‹ add garlic, ginger and spices. Sauté 5 minutes. Add eggplant, tomatoes and salt. Sauté 5 minutes. Cover and simmer on low heat ½ hour, stirring often to prevent sticking.

Three Bean Dal

Kidney, black and aduki beans work well together in this special dal. _Note that the beans need to be soaked overnight, so plan accordingly._

· SERVES 6-8 ·

1 cup Kidney beans
1 cup black beans
1 cup azuki beans (or adzuki beans) — _found at natural food stores_
9 cups water
1 tsp. fennel seed
1 tsp. coriander seed
1 tsp. cumin seed
1 tsp. mustard seed
2 Tbsp. canola oil
1 large onion, chopped
5 large cloves garlic, pressed
3 Tbsp. freshly grated ginger
salt

Rinse beans and pick through. Put all beans in a large bowl. Add water to cover by 2". Cover and let sit out overnight.

Drain off water the next day, and place beans in a large pot with 9 cups of fresh water. Cover and bring to a boil. Reduce heat and simmer for 1 hour.

Meanwhile, roast seeds by placing all the seeds into a dry skillet, and toast on a low heat for 5 to 7 minutes, or till fragrant. Grind either in a mortar and pestle, or in an electric coffee grinder. Add to beans.

In the same skillet, heat oil ⌐ add onion & garlic ⌐ sauté 7 minutes. Add to beans, along with ginger and some salt. Cover & simmer for 1 hour.

Remove cover and mash beans a bit with a potato masher (they won't all mash totally). Cook, uncovered, on a low heat for 1 hour, stirring often. Serve.

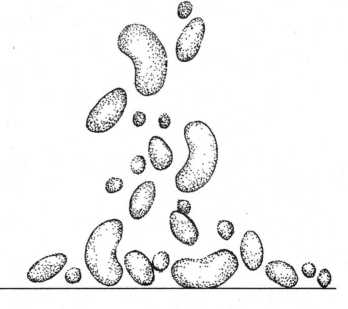

Vegetable Sushi

Especially special on a hot summer day — accompanied by a salad tossed with _Japanese Ginger Dressing_.
... this is a very difficult recipe to put into words, so please bear with me while I try to explain how to do this.

· SERVES 4 ·

1 cup sushi rice
1½ cups water
¼ cup sesame seeds, roasted
12 sheets of nori
¼ cup umeboshi paste
2 oz. pickled ginger
6 scallions, cut into thin strips (use greens)
2 small cucumbers, peeled & cut into long thin strips

1 avocado, peeled & cut into long thin strips

Cook rice early in the day to allow it to cool — place rice in a strainer and run under cold water for several minutes... shake out excess water... place into a small pot and add water. Cover and bring to a boil... reduce heat to low and cook, covered, for 15 minutes. Set aside to cool for several hours.

To roast sesame seeds... place them in a dry skillet and brown lightly on a low heat. This takes only minutes, so

Keep your eye on them to prevent burning.

Have all the remaining ingredients ready to roll (that may have been a bad cooking pun... as in sushi roll... no?...)

Now, to get serious... If you have a sushi mat, get it out. If not, don't worry... as I have one but never use it. Place a sheet of nori on sushi mat or cutting board. Spread 3 Tbsp. rice evenly over the entire nori surface. Take about ½ tsp. umeboshi paste and spread on the rice ⌐ then take a few slivers of pickled ginger and place down the center of rice (lengthwise). Now, place a long strip of scallion greens, a cucumber strip or two, and a strip of avocado all going down the center (again, lengthwise).

Sprinkle with a ½ tsp. of roasted sesame seeds, and roll up like a jelly roll. Using a sharp knife, slice the roll into 6 even pieces.

Repeat again and again with all the remaining ingredients. ⌐ Good luck!

   ... boy, if I would have realized how difficult
   it was to explain all this, I may have
   skipped the recipe entirely!! ...

Japanese Hot Pot

A large steaming pot of broth filled with noodles...veggies...tofu.
You can add or substitute shrimp or chicken ~ very soothing.

· SERVES 4-6 ·

1.5 oz. dried shiitake mushrooms
½ cup arame seaweed ~ found at
            natural food stores
2 cups hot water
2 Tbsp. freshly grated ginger
2 cloves garlic, pressed
2 Tbsp. dried bonito flakes-
                optional
2 Tbsp. roasted sesame oil
12 cups water
3 Tbsp. mirin

3 Tbsp. tamari
½ tsp. hot red pepper flakes
                 (optional)
1 head bok choy, chopped
1 bunch scallions
2 carrots, cut into rounds
1 lb. firm tofu, cubed
1 lb. soba or udon noodles
(linguine also substitutes nicely)
½ cup mellow white miso

Place shiitake mushrooms & arame into a bowl ~ cover
with hot water & set aside to soak for 30 minutes. Place
all the remaining ingredients (except for miso & noodles)
into a large soup pot. Cover & bring to a boil. Reduce
heat & simmer 30 minutes. Add shiitake mushrooms,
arame & soaking liquid to pot. Cover & simmer for 20
minutes. Meanwhile cook noodles as directed on package. While the soup is simmering and noodles are being
cooked, remove 2 cups of broth from pot ~ add miso ~
mix well & return to pot. Drain noodles ~ add to pot & mix.

Rena's Black Beans and Rice

Rena lived in San Cristóbal de las Casas in Chiapas, Mexico...
and has never been the same again! Because of the beautiful
fresh produce there, she did manage to learn some cooking!!

· SERVES 4-6 ·

2 cups brown rice
3 Tbsp. olive oil
1 large Spanish onion, chopped
7 large cloves garlic, pressed
2 green bell peppers, cored, seeded & chopped
2 carrots, sliced
10 fresh tomatoes, chopped
2 jalapeno peppers ⁓ cored, seeded & chopped
(optional)
2 16-oz. cans black beans
2 tsp. cumin powder
salt to taste

Cook rice as directed. While rice is cooking, heat olive oil
in a large skillet ⁓ add onion and garlic ⁓ sauté for
5 minutes. Add peppers and carrots ⁓ sauté 7 minutes.
Add tomatoes, jalapeno peppers, black beans, cumin,
and some salt.

Cover and simmer for 45 minutes. Serve over rice. ♡

⁓ Que Sabroso!

Spinach Enchiladas with Tomatillo Sauce

The piquant flavors of the tomatillo sauce pair well with the smoothness of the enchiladas ... a winner!

• SERVES 6-8 •

3 lbs. fresh spinach — wash well, discard coarse stems & chop
¼ cup water
3 Tbsp. olive oil
3 leeks — wash well, discard tough part & chop
3 large cloves garlic, pressed
1 Tbsp. ground cumin
1 cup canned diced chilies
¼ cup fresh cilantro, chopped
1 cup sour cream
salt to taste
8 oz. sharp cheddar cheese
8 oz. Monterey Jack cheese
12 -14 flour or corn tortillas

Place spinach in a large pot & add water. Cover and bring to a boil. Reduce heat & cook for 5 minutes. Remove spinach from pot & drain well in colander. Set aside. In a large skillet heat olive oil ⁓ add leeks & garlic ⁓ sauté 8 minutes. Add cumin, chilies, cilantro, sour cream & a little salt. Mix well. Add spinach & 4 oz. of cheddar & 4 oz. of jack cheese ... save the rest for later. Mix well. Set aside as you make Tomatillo Sauce

Tomatillo Sauce

¼ cup olive oil
1 onion, chopped
3 cloves garlic, pressed
2 13-oz. cans tomatillos, chopped
1 cup chicken or vegetable broth
2 Tbsp. ground cumin
¼ cup fresh cilantro, chopped
salt to taste

Heat oil in a large pot—add onion & garlic. Sauté on a low heat 10 minutes. Add tomatillos, broth, cumin, cilantro & salt. Cover & bring to a boil. Reduce heat to low & simmer for 30 minutes, stirring often.

To assemble the enchiladas ~ pour ½ of the tomatillo sauce into a large baking dish. Lay tortilla on a cutting board & spoon 3 heaping Tbsp's. of spinach filling onto the middle of tortilla. Roll up like a jelly roll. Place the stuffed tortilla, seam side down, in the baking dish. Continue doing this with all the tortillas and filling. Preheat the oven to 350°.

Pour the remaining tomatillo sauce over the enchiladas and sprinkle remaining cheese on top. Bake at 350° for ½ hour & serve. Chopped fresh cilantro makes a nice garnish.

Nana Irene's Pierogi

...an old world blend of Polish & Russian cuisine, nestled in the heart of Binghamton! ♥ ♡ ♥ ♡ ♥

• MAKES 30 PIEROGI •

POTATO FILLING:

2 large potatoes, peeled & diced
¼ tsp. salt
2 oz. cheddar cheese, grated
1 Tbsp. butter

DOUGH:

1 egg
½ cup water
2 cups flour
¼ cup safflower oil

ONION TOPPING:

4 Tbsp. butter
2 large onions, sliced
salt & pepper to taste

Make filling... place potatoes in a pot & cover with water. Cover & bring to a boil. Cook for 10 minutes or till tender. Drain in colander. Return to pot & mash with a potato masher. Add salt, cheese & butter. Mix well. Cover & set aside as you make dough. Beat eggs with water in a bowl. Add flour & mix well. Add oil & mix well. Remove from bowl & knead until satiny smooth. Roll out on floured surface until thin ~ cut into 2x2" squares. Place 1 tsp. filling onto each square ~ fold in half, making a rectangle. Pinch edges well to keep filling inside. Bring a large pot of water to a boil ~ drop pierogi into boiling water & cook until they rise to the top. Then cook 5 minutes longer. While pierogi are cooking, make onion topping. Melt butter in a large skillet ~ add sliced onions and sauté 10 minutes or till browned. Add salt & pepper to taste. If timing is good, the pierogi are ready to drain in colander. Run cold water over to remove starch (but not to cool). Place in a bowl ~ spoon onions over top and serve.

Spinach Kugel

This is a great old Jewish noodle recipe that probably dates back to the days of Moses. Moses most likely used fresh spinach instead of frozen... and I'm not certain that he was able to get his hands on dried onion soup mix! It tastes great ~ feeds the masses ~ and the kids love it.

· SERVES 6-8 ·

2 10-oz. boxes of frozen chopped spinach
1 lb. wide flat noodles (ribbons)
2 eggs
1 pkg. dried onion soup mix (1.4 oz.) ~ look for Mayacamas
                                        at health food or gourmet stores
1 cup sour cream
4 Tbsp. butter

Preheat oven to 350° Butter a large baking dish. Cook spinach as directed on package, and at the same time begin cooking noodles as directed. Meanwhile, beat eggs in a bowl ~ add onion soup and sour cream, and mix very well, making sure there are no onion soup lumps lurking around. Set aside.

Drain the noodles in a colander ~ put back into pot and add butter. Mix to melt. Set aside as you drain the spinach well in the same colander. Add spinach to noodles and mix. Add egg mixture and mix well. Spoon noodle mixture into buttered baking dish and bake at 350° for 30 minutes.

Lentil Loaf

Serve with Mushroom Gravy & mashed potatoes for a down-home vegetarian meal.

· SERVES 4-6 ·

2 cups brown lentils
6 cups water
1 cup brown rice
2 cups water
3 Tbsp. canola oil
1 large onion,
    finely chopped

3 large cloves garlic, pressed
2 celery ribs, finely chopped
2 carrots, grated
¼ cup fresh thyme, chopped
        (important)
1 egg, beaten (optional)
salt & pepper to taste

Place lentils in a pot with 6 cups water. Cover & bring to a boil. Reduce heat & cook on low for 1 hour, or till lentils are soft. Water should be absorbed, but if not, drain lentils & discard extra water. While lentils are cooking, the rice should also be cooking... rinse rice & place in a pot with 2 cups water. Cover & bring to a boil. Reduce heat & simmer on low for 30 minutes. Mix the lentils & rice together in a large bowl. Set aside. Preheat oven to 350°. Oil a bread pan or small baking dish. Heat oil in a large skillet. Add onion & garlic – sauté 5 minutes. Add celery, carrots & thyme – sauté 3 minutes. Add to lentils and rice – mix well. Add egg, salt and pepper – mix well. Form into a loaf & place in pan. Bake at 350° for 1 hour. While the lentil loaf is baking, you may wish to make the mushroom gravy (pg. 133).

Mushroom Gravy

I made this gravy one Thanksgiving to be served over a lentil loaf and mashed potatoes for the strict vegetarians in the family. It turned out so well that even the not-strictly vegetarians loved it!

• MAKES APPROXIMATELY 5-6 CUPS GRAVY •

3 Tbsp. olive oil
3 leeks, rinsed & chopped (discard tough parts of stems)
1 large clove garlic, pressed
1 lb. mushrooms, sliced
3 Tbsp. sherry
½ cup nutritional yeast
½ cup flour
3 Tbsp. tamari
5 cups water
salt & pepper to taste

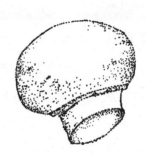

Heat oil in a skillet – add leeks and garlic – sauté 5 minutes. Add mushrooms & sauté 5 minutes. Add sherry, yeast and flour – mix well to form a roux. Add tamari, water, and salt & pepper.

Simmer, uncovered, on a low heat for ½ hour, stirring often to prevent sticking.

Rice and Veggies

Rice and Veggies...a broad term covering so many combinations of ingredients ... always different each time it's made. It's simple, nourishing and comforting. Serve with a green salad for a healthful, delicious meal.

· SERVES 4 ·

1½ cups long or short grain brown rice
3 cups water
2 Tbsp. safflower oil
1 Tbsp. roasted sesame oil
3 large cloves garlic, pressed
2 Tbsp. freshly grated ginger
1 bunch scallions, chopped
2 carrots, coarsely chopped
1 celery rib, coarsely chopped
1 small bok choy, coarsely chopped
½ lb. fresh shiitake mushrooms
2 Tbsp. tamari
1 Tbsp. curry powder

Rinse rice under cold water and drain. Place in a medium-size pot. Add water – cover and bring to a boil. Reduce heat to low, and cook, covered, for ½ hour. Shut off heat and let rice sit (I like to cook the rice early in the day, as it dries out to a perfect consistency as it sits).

Heat oils in a wok or a large cast iron skillet (or whatever). Add garlic and ginger – stir-fry 1 minute. Add all the remaining veggies, and stir-fry 5 minutes. Add tamari and curry powder, and stir-fry another 5 minutes.

Add rice to wok. Stir-fry for 5 minutes or until the rice is heated through, and serve.

Bombay Vegetable Curry

Serve with brown basmati rice, Cucumber Raita, & Mango Chutney.

• SERVES 6-8 •

2 cups uncooked brown basmati rice
4 cups water
4 Tbsp. butter or 4 Tbsp. canola oil or
    2 Tbsp. butter and 2 Tbsp. canola oil
5 large cloves garlic, pressed
2 Tbsp. freshly grated ginger
1 red onion, chopped
2 Tbsp. curry powder
2 Tbsp. cumin powder
2 Tbsp. garam masala ~ optional
1 tsp. ground coriander
¼ cup fresh cilantro, chopped
2 cups canned tomatoes
4 large potatoes, cut into bite-size pieces
1 large cauliflower, broken into florets
salt to taste
1 cup water
2 cups fresh or frozen peas

Rinse rice under cold water several times, shake out excess water, place in a pot and add 4 cups water. Cover and bring to a boil — reduce heat & cook on a low heat for 40 minutes.

Melt butter in a large skillet — add garlic, ginger and onion — sauté 5 minutes. Add spices and mix well. Add cilantro, tomatoes, potatoes, cauliflower, salt, and water. Mix well. Cover and simmer on a medium-low heat for 30 minutes or until veggies are tender. Add peas — cover and simmer 7 minutes.

Serve over rice.

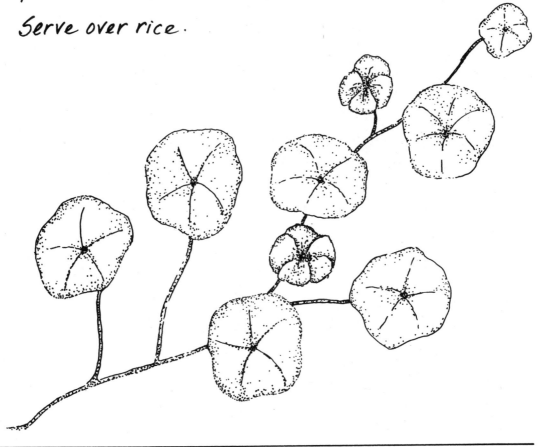

Dal

Dal is a traditional Indian dish. Serve with brown basmati rice, Vegetable Korma and Cucumber Raita for a hearty & satisfying meal.

· SERVES 6-8 ·

3 cups red lentils ⁓ found at natural food
8 cups water   stores or at Indian markets
3 Tbsp. canola oil
1 large onion, chopped
3 large cloves garlic, pressed
1 Tbsp. ground fennel seed
1 Tbsp. ground cumin seed
1 Tbsp. panchpuran ⁓ optional
1 Tbsp. freshly grated ginger
salt to taste

Rinse lentils well. Place in a pot with 8 cups water. Cover & bring to a boil. Reduce heat & simmer.

Meanwhile, heat oil in a skillet. Add onion, garlic, ground seeds, and ginger ⁓ sauté 10 minutes. Add skillet contents to lentils, along with a little salt. Stir well. Cover and simmer on a low heat for 1½ hours, stirring often to prevent sticking.

Serve hot with rice.

<u>Love and Mike's Spicy Stir-Fry</u>

... with chicken ... or tofu ... or all veggies

· SERVES 4 ·

2 cups brown rice
1 whole boneless chicken breast
4 Tbsp. canola oil
3 tsp. curry powder
1 tsp. black pepper
1 tsp. paprika
2 Tbsp. tamari
2 large cloves garlic, pressed
½ large onion, chopped
2 carrots, chopped
1 red or green bell pepper, chopped
½ head broccoli, broken into florets
½ head cauliflower, broken into florets
½ zucchini, chopped
½ yellow squash, chopped

Prepare rice as directed. Meanwhile rinse chicken – pat dry & cut into bite-size pieces. Heat 2 Tbsp. oil in a wok or large skillet – add chicken, 1 tsp. curry powder, ½ tsp. black pepper, ½ tsp. paprika & 1 Tbsp. tamari – stir-fry 5 minutes. Remove from pan & set aside. In same wok or skillet, heat remaining 2 Tbsp. oil – add garlic & onion – stir-fry 1 minute. Add remaining veggies & spices – stir-fry 5 minutes. Add chicken & remaining Tbsp. of tamari – stir-fry 10 minutes. Add rice – mix well – stir-fry 3 minutes & serve. ♡ ♡ ♡ ♡ ♡ ♡ ♡

Mary's Portobello Stuffed Peppers

⌐ Mary is not only a great cook, but a great artist too!

· SERVES 4-6 ·

1½ cups uncooked rice
10 large green or red bell peppers, cored & seeded (cut off tops)
3 Tbsp. olive oil
1 large onion, chopped
2 celery ribs, chopped
12 oz. Portobello mushrooms
½ cup fresh parsley, chopped
½ cup fresh dill, chopped
¼ cup freshly grated Romano cheese
Salt & pepper to taste
1 28-oz. can crushed tomatoes

Begin cooking rice as directed. Meanwhile, bring 2 quarts of water to a boil. Blanch peppers in water for 2 minutes & drain. Set aside to cool. Preheat oven to 350°. Heat oil in a skillet ⌐ add onion & celery ⌐ sauté 3 minutes. Add mushrooms & cook on a medium/high heat for 5 minutes. Place rice into a bowl ⌐ add skillet contents & mix. Add herbs, cheese, and salt & pepper to taste. Mix well. Spoon mixture into peppers. Pour crushed tomatoes into a large baking dish & stand peppers in sauce. Spoon a little sauce over each pepper. Bake at 350° for 45-50 minutes, basting with sauce every 15 minutes. Serve with garlic bread, a green salad and a glass of red wine. ♡

Savory Swiss Chard Pie

Pie Crust for a 9" pie (see page 217)

2 Tbsp. olive oil
1 large clove garlic, pressed
½ large Spanish onion, chopped
1 lb. Swiss chard, washed & chopped
3 Tbsp. fresh sweet marjoram
3 large eggs
½ cup Half & Half or milk
salt & pepper to taste
¼ lb. Provolone cheese, sliced
¼ cup freshly grated Parmesan cheese
paprika

Preheat oven to 350°. Make pie crust as directed &
set aside. Heat olive oil in a skillet ~ add garlic &
onion ~ sauté 5 minutes. Add chard & marjoram ~
sauté 5 minutes. Beat eggs and Half & Half together in a bowl. Add salt & pepper ~ set aside. Add
Provolone cheese to chard mixture and mix well.
Add egg mixture & mix well. Spoon into prepared pie
crust. Sprinkle Parmesan cheese evenly over top &
then dust with a little paprika. Bake at 350° for
40 minutes. Serve immediately.

Carol's Enchirritos

↪ a yummy Tex-Mex creation

· SERVES 6 ·

2 Tbsp. olive oil
1 lb. ground turkey
1 red bell pepper, chopped
1 medium onion, chopped
3 large cloves garlic, pressed
1 tsp. cumin powder
1 tsp. chili powder
Tabasco sauce to taste
1½ cup salsa
6 8" whole wheat or white flour tortillas
½ lb. low-fat Monterey Jack cheese, grated

Heat 1 Tbsp. oil in a large skillet. Add turkey & sauté for 7 minutes. Remove from pan & set aside. Add remaining Tbsp. of oil to same skillet. Add peppers, onion & garlic – sauté 5 minutes. Add turkey, cumin, chili powder, Tabasco sauce & ½ cup salsa. Mix well. Remove from heat. Oil a medium baking dish & preheat oven to 350°. To assemble, put ⅙ turkey mixture in center of 1 tortilla, top with 2 Tbsp. cheese, roll up & place in baking dish seam side down. Repeat with remaining tortillas. Place filled tortillas close together in baking dish. Top with remaining salsa & cheese.
Bake at 350° for 20 minutes till hot and bubbly.

Vegetable Curry

~ exotic!

· SERVES 4-6 ·

2 cups brown or white basmati rice

2 Tbsp. butter or safflower oil

1 medium yellow onion, chopped

3 large cloves garlic, pressed

2 Tbsp. freshly grated ginger

3 Tbsp. curry powder

2 Tbsp. ground cumin seed

1 Tbsp. ground fennel seed

1 Tbsp. tamarind paste ~ optional

juice of ½ lime

1 cup water

2 cups crushed tomatoes

3 Tbsp. tamari

1 head broccoli, broken into florets

7 small red potatoes, chopped

2 carrots, cut into rounds

½ cup raisins

1 apple, chopped

1 cup plain yogurt

2 Tbsp. honey

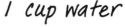

Begin cooking rice as directed (I like to cook it a little earlier in the day & let it sit as it dries out somewhat, which I prefer).

Melt butter in a large skillet. Add onion, garlic, ginger and spices. Cook 10 minutes on a low heat, stirring often. Add tamarind paste, lime juice, water, crushed tomatoes and tamari. Simmer 5 minutes. Add veggies, raisins and apple. Cover & cook on low 15 minutes, stirring often. Add yogurt & honey. Mix well. Cook 5 minutes. Serve over rice.

Little Vegetable Dishes

Garlic Roasted Potatoes

Unbeatable! A must try... you'll love them with chicken or fish, or as a highlight to a vegetarian meal... not to mention how they can transform a bowl of pesto into the incredible Pesto Genovese!

· SERVES 4-6 ·

12 medium red potatoes, scrubbed & quartered
¼ cup olive oil
6 large cloves garlic, pressed
salt & pepper

Preheat oven to 350°. Prepare the potatoes & set aside.

Put olive oil, garlic & a decent amount of salt & pepper into a bowl. Mix. Place a few pieces of potato into the oil mixture & roll around to coat a little. Place into an ungreased baking pan. Repeat till all the potatoes are coated.

Cover baking pan & bake at 350° for 30 minutes. Remove cover, flip the potatoes over with a spatula, and bake uncovered for 60 minutes, flipping them again after 30 minutes.

Stir-Fry Snow Peas

These snow peas went right from my garden into the wok.

· SERVES 4-6 ·

1 lb. snow peas — rinse & remove stem
2 Tbsp. canola oil
3 large cloves garlic, pressed
3 Tbsp. hoison sauce
1 Tbsp. tamari

Prepare snow peas and set aside while you heat oil in a wok or large skillet.

Add garlic & stir-fry 1 minute ... add snow peas & stir-fry 3 minutes. Add hoison sauce & tamari & stir-fry 2 minutes.

Serve.

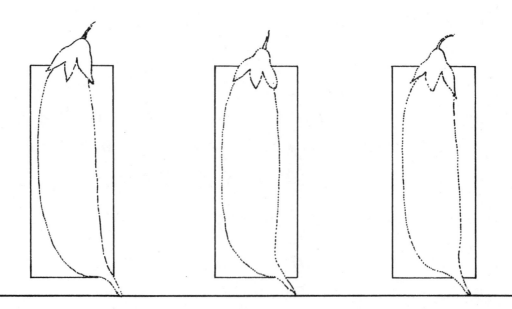

Brussels Sprouts and Carrots

Brussels Sprouts have a bad name. Part of the problem lies in the horrid odor they exude when steamed. It's a shame, as they're really a charming vegetable. I found that there is no nasty odor when they're sautéed... really. Try them, as they are in the cabbage family... the friendly vegetables that help keep us cute and healthy!

· SERVES 4-6 ·

2 Tbsp. butter or olive oil or 1 Tbsp. butter & 1 Tbsp. olive oil

1 lb. Brussels sprouts, cut in half if smallish or into thirds if large-ish

3 carrots, peeled & julienned

juice of 1 lemon

2 Tbsp. water

salt & pepper to taste

Prepare the Brussels sprouts and carrots, and set aside as you melt butter in a large skillet. Put in sprouts and carrots — sauté 7 minutes. Squeeze lemon over top and add water.

Cover and cook on a low fire for 7-10 minutes, or until sprouts and carrots are tender... do not overcook.

Season with salt & pepper — mix and serve.

Zucchini and Sun-Dried Tomatoes

This is a great little dish ⁓ it's even better the next day.

• SERVES 4 •

3 Tbsp. olive oil
3 large cloves garlic, pressed
3 large sun-dried tomatoes (packed in oil)
⁓ drain and cut into strips
4 small zucchini, cut into thin strips
1 ripe tomato, chopped
¼ cup dry white or red wine
Salt & pepper to taste
¼ cup freshly grated Parmesan cheese

Heat oil in a large skillet. Add garlic and sun-dried tomatoes ⁓ sauté 3 minutes. Add zucchini & tomato, and sauté 5 minutes. Add wine and a little salt & pepper. Cover and simmer 5 minutes, or until zucchini is tender yet firm.

Remove from stove ⁓ add cheese ⁓ cover and let sit 3 minutes... then serve.

Joan's Zesty Carrots

• SERVES 4 •

6-8 large carrots, julienned
water
2 Tbsp. grated onion
2 Tbsp. prepared white horseradish
$\frac{1}{2}$ cup mayonnaise
$\frac{1}{2}$ tsp. salt
$\frac{1}{4}$ tsp. pepper
$\frac{1}{4}$ cup unseasoned bread crumbs
2 Tbsp. butter, cut into little pieces

Place carrots into a pot — add 1" water. Cover and steam for 7 minutes or till tender/firm (is there such a thing?). Drain.

Preheat oven to 375°. Butter a shallow casserole dish — spoon carrots into dish & set aside.

Mix onion, horseradish, mayo, salt, and pepper together. Spoon over carrots. Sprinkle evenly with bread crumbs & dot with butter.

Bake at 375° for 15 minutes.

Different!

Skillet Browned Potatoes

A perfect match for chicken or fish... or serve as a main feature with other vegetarian dishes. Also good as a breakfast potato.

· SERVES 4-6 ·

14 Yukon Gold potatoes (or all-purpose potatoes)
Water
Olive oil
3 large cloves garlic, pressed
2 Tbsp. dried parsley
Salt & pepper to taste

Early in the day, or at least 1 hour before starting dinner, place potatoes in a pot & cover with water. Cover & bring to a boil. Reduce heat & simmer for 20 minutes, or till potatoes are slightly tender, but still quite firm when pierced with a fork. Drain in a colander & set aside to cool. When potatoes are cool & dinner is being prepared, slice potatoes into thick rounds. Heat enough olive oil to coat a large skillet, and add garlic. Sauté 1 minute (if your skillet isn't large enough to hold all the potatoes at one time, then cook in two shifts, using half of the oil, garlic, etc. each time). Add potatoes in a single layer. Sprinkle with parsley flakes, salt and pepper. Cook on medium heat for approximately 10 minutes, or till browned. Flip over and cook another 10 minutes ⌣ serve.

Basmati Rice With Snow Peas

Aromatic basmati rice made even more delightful by the addition of steamed snow peas.

· SERVES 4-6 ·

2 cups basmati rice
1 cup chicken or vegetable broth
2 cups water
½ lb. snow peas — remove stems

Rinse rice well under cold water & drain excess water. Place in a pot — add broth and water. Cover and bring to a boil. Reduce heat to low, and simmer 15 minutes. Remove from heat — place snow peas on top of rice. Cover and let sit 5 minutes. Serve.

— great with grilled fish or chicken

Broccoli Rabe

I have a confession to make... I am not a big fan of Broccoli Rabe. I'm beginning to believe that one must be Italian to really love this vegetable. Or if you _are_ Italian, you could never admit to _not_ liking it! I've tried it several times, but it just does not send me. Why then am I including it in this book, you might ask? I do know people (mostly Italian) who love it (or at least say that they do!), and I thought I shouldn't let my prejudice keep others from enjoying it. Good luck!

· SERVES 2 to 4 ·

1 bunch broccoli rabe, coarsely chopped (remove and discard tough stems)
2 Tbsp. olive oil
3 large cloves garlic, pressed
¼ cup water
salt & pepper to taste
juice of 1 lemon

Heat olive oil in a large skillet — add garlic & sauté 1 minute. Add broccoli rabe & sauté 5 minutes. Add water. Cover and cook on a medium heat for 7 minutes, or until all the water is absorbed. Season with salt & pepper. Squeeze lemon over top, mix all together and serve.

Cauliflower & Carrot Dijon

~ Great combo!

• SERVES 4-6 •

1 Tbsp. butter
1 Tbsp. olive oil
2 large cloves garlic, pressed
1 small onion, chopped
1 head cauliflower, trimmed & cut into florets
3 large carrots, peeled & julienned
1 tsp. dried basil
1 tsp. dried tarragon
3 Tbsp. Dijon mustard
$\frac{1}{8}$ cup dry white wine
$\frac{1}{8}$ cup water
salt & pepper to taste

Melt butter in a large skillet. Add olive oil, garlic and onion. Sauté 7 minutes. Add cauliflower, carrots and herbs ~ sauté for 5 minutes. Add mustard, wine, water, and salt & pepper. Mix well. Cover and simmer on a low heat for 10 minutes, stirring often. Cook until veggies are tender, but do not overcook.

Roasted Root Vegetables

a winner... easy... a must try! Also quite a tongue twister ~ try saying it 10 times real fast...

• SERVES... well, you determine that...!

CHOOSE SOME OR ALL OF THE FOLLOWING:

yams	parsnips
carrots	celery
potatoes	fennel
garlic	leeks
onion	turnips
beets	shallots

let your imagination run wild!

AND DON'T FORGET:

olive oil and salt & pepper

Preheat oven to 350°. Here is what you do ~ prepare veggies of choice by peeling & cutting into large pieces. Place the veggies into a large bowl ~ drizzle liberally with olive oil ~ add some salt & pepper, and mix well. Place veggies into an oiled baking pan.
Cover and bake at 350° for 40 minutes ~ then uncover and bake for an additional 30 minutes. Serve.

Sautéed Escarole

One of my most favorite greens ... escarole is in the endive family, but has a milder flavor than Belgian or curly endive. Escarole is also delicious when young & tender, added to a salad. It's also loaded with essential vitamins and minerals.

· SERVES 4 ·

1 large head escarole, coarsely chopped (rinse well)
2 Tbsp. olive oil
3 large cloves garlic, pressed
1 Tbsp. balsamic vinegar
salt & pepper to taste

Drain off any excess water from escarole. Heat oil in a large skillet ‒ add garlic, and sauté 1 minute. Add escarole and sauté 10 minutes. Add vinegar, and salt & pepper to taste.

Mix well and serve.

Mashed Sweet Potatoes

This certainly is not an earth-shattering recipe, but I think it's great, and maybe you haven't thought of the idea. Try to find Garnet Yams, as they are sweet... and beautiful to look at. Sweet potatoes and yams are loaded with vitamin A ~~and~~ vitamin C.

· SERVES 4 ·

5 large sweet potatoes or yams
water
3 Tbsp. butter
juice of 1 orange or $\frac{1}{4}$ cup OJ
$\frac{1}{4}$ cup milk
salt to taste

Peel potatoes and cut into pieces. Place in a large pot & cover with water. Cover & bring to a boil. Cook about 20 minutes, or until potatoes are tender when pricked with a fork. Drain off water. Mash with a potato masher. Add butter... Keep mashing... add orange juice, milk, and salt to taste... mashing all the while.

Whisk the potatoes a bit with a wire whisk until nice and smooth.

Serve immediately.

Broccoli and/or Cauliflower with Cheese Sauce

Yes, I do realize that most of you know how to make a cheese sauce... and probably even know how to steam veggies! And most know how to pour the cheese sauce over the veggies...! But what if there are those who _don't_ know, or, for that matter, some may welcome the suggestion when they are pulling out their hair for lack of ideas.

· SERVES 4-6 ·

1 large head broccoli _or_ cauliflower ~~or~~
    ½ head broccoli _and_ ½ head cauliflower
          ~ broken into florets

2 Tbsp. butter
1 small clove garlic, pressed
1 Tbsp. Dijon mustard
1 Tbsp. flour
1 cup milk
1 cup grated sharp cheddar cheese

Prepare the broccoli and/or cauliflower ~ place into a pot with 1" of water... cover & steam for 7 minutes. While the veggies are steaming, melt butter in a medium pot. Add garlic, mustard & flour ~ mix to make a roux. Slowly add milk, whisking with a wire whisk as you do. Heat on a low heat for 5 minutes. Add cheese and mix well. Drain the veggies... place into a bowl... pour cheese sauce over top and serve.

Baked Beans

Baking beans is a very cozy thing to do when it is cold and miserable outside... and you welcome the heat the oven provides, along with the wonderful aroma that fills the house. The oven is on for 3 hours, so you may wish to roast a chicken to serve with the beans... or perhaps bake a cake for dessert.
Please note that the beans must be soaked overnight, so plan accordingly.

· SERVES 6-8 ·

1 lb. dry Great Northern beans
water to cover for soaking... plus
10 cups of water for cooking
1 large onion, chopped
3 large cloves garlic, pressed
1 cup light brown sugar
¼ cup maple syrup
½ cup Ketchup
¼ cup Dijon mustard
juice of 1 lemon
3 Tbsp. blackstrap molasses
2 Tbsp. Worcestershire sauce
1 tsp. salt

Place beans in a large pot and cover with water. Cover and let soak overnight.

In the morning, drain off excess soaking water. Put the beans back into the pot and add 10 cups fresh water.

Cover and bring to a boil. Reduce heat and simmer, covered, for 2 hours. Remove from heat and carefully pour beans ~ with liquid ~ into a bean pot or a covered casserole dish. Add remaining ingredients and mix well.

Cover and bake at 350° for 3 hours, stirring every 30 minutes.

Broccoli Sesame

~ one of our favorite ways to eat this important veggie.

· SERVES 4 ·

  1 large head broccoli, cut into florets
  juice of 1 lemon
  1 Tbsp. tamari
  1 Tbsp. toasted sesame seeds

Place broccoli florets into a pot ~ add 1" water. Cover and steam 5 minutes.

While the broccoli is steaming, toast seeds by placing into a dry skillet and cook on a medium heat till golden. This takes only a few minutes, so be attentive.

Remove broccoli from pot ~ place into a bowl & squeeze lemon juice over top. Drizzle tamari evenly over top as well.

Sprinkle with sesame seeds and serve.

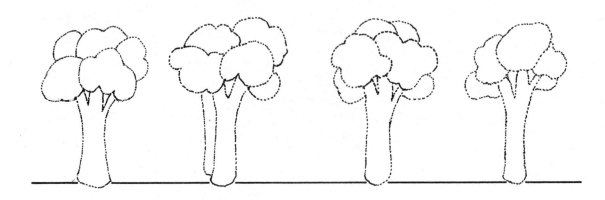

Scalloped Potatoes

Butter! Milk! Fat...Fat...Fat!! Sometimes you just have to throw caution to the wind!

· SERVES 6-8 ·

5 lbs. all-purpose potatoes, scrubbed & cut into thin rounds
(leave skins on, or remove, if you prefer)
4 Tbsp. butter
2 Tbsp. Dijon mustard
3 Tbsp. finely chopped onion
3 Tbsp. flour
salt & pepper to taste
6 cups milk
paprika

Preheat oven to 350°. Butter a 11 x 14-inch baking pan, and place cut potatoes into baking pan. Melt butter in a medium/largish pot. Add mustard and onion — sauté 3 minutes. Add flour, salt and pepper. Stir to form a roux. Slowly add milk while whisking the mixture with a wire whisk... cooking on a low fire for 5 minutes.

Pour the butter/milk mixture over the potatoes in pan and sprinkle liberally with paprika.

Cover and bake at 350° for 20 minutes. Uncover and bake an additional 45 minutes.

Broiled Vegetables

In the summer time when fresh tomatoes are deliciously available, try broiling veggies. They are quite different from grilled vegetables as all the juices blend together to make a great saucy dish. They are wonderful served alone or with chicken or fish. They are terrific piled on a good bread topped with a sun-dried tomato or two.

· SERVES 4 to 6 ·

1 medium yellow summer squash
1 medium green zucchini squash
2 large red onions
4 large fresh tomatoes
12 large cloves garlic, peeled
1 large red bell pepper
1 Hungarian hot-waxed pepper (optional)
¼ cup olive oil
juice of 1 lemon
salt & pepper to taste

Cut all the veggies into large pieces — leave the garlic cloves whole. Place vegetables in a large bowl — add olive oil, lemon, salt & pepper. Mix well. Transfer to a large broiling pan. Place in oven about 4 to 6 inches from top broiler flame. Broil about 10 minutes, then mix as well as possible and broil another 10 minutes.

Spoon veggies & juices into a serving bowl and serve.

Fish & Seafood

Denise's Grilled Yellowtail Snapper with a Warm Mango Avocado Salsa

Denise created this dish while vacationing in the Florida Keys, where yellowtail snapper is abundant. If you can't find yellowtail, then red snapper will do nicely.

· SERVES 4 ·

2 lbs. yellowtail snapper fillets
2 Tbsp. olive oil

SALSA

2 small Haas avocados, peeled and cubed

2 small or 1 large ripe mango, peeled & cubed

¼ cup fresh cilantro, chopped

1 tsp. palm sugar or light brown sugar

¼ cup lime juice

salt & pepper to taste

1 small Thai hot pepper, seeded & chopped ~ optional

2 Tbsp. butter

Prepare the grill. While grill is heating up, place fish fillets on a plate and drizzle with olive oil. Set aside.

Meanwhile, mix all the salsa ingredients together (except for butter) in a bowl. Set aside.

When grill is hot, grill fish for approximately 3 minutes per side. As soon as you place the fish on the grill, melt butter in a pan ~ add prepared salsa and sauté on medium heat for 3 minutes (hopefully someone is tending the fish while you heat the salsa!). Place fish on a platter ~ spoon salsa over top and serve.

Thai Fish Cakes

This may be the only real fried recipe in the book... but it is worth making an exception for ~ Must be served with Thai Cucumber Salad.

· SERVES 4 ·

2 lb. catfish fillets
2 eggs
½ cup chopped fresh cilantro
1 Tbsp. red curry paste
2 Tbsp. fish sauce
½ cup water
peanut oil for frying

Put all of the above ingredients (except for the oil) into a food processor or blender, and whirl till well mixed. Remove from processor and place into a bowl. Form into patties (wet hands before making each patty) and set aside.

Put 1" of peanut oil in bottom of a cast iron skillet and heat. When hot, place as many fish cakes in pan as will fit without crowding. Fry on a medium heat till golden brown ~ then flip cakes and fry on other side. Remove from pan, drain on several layers of paper towels and serve with cucumber salad.

Swordfish with Green Olives and Garlic
Great!

· SERVES 4 ·

2 lbs. swordfish
1 tbsp. olive oil
juice of 1 lemon
salt & pepper
14 large green olives, chopped – stuffed with pimento

3 large cloves garlic, pressed

Place swordfish steaks onto a broiling pan and drizzle with olive oil. Squeeze lemon juice over top, and sprinkle with a little salt & pepper. Mix chopped olives and pressed garlic together on a cutting board. Take a sharp knife and chop them as fine as you can to form a coarse paste (if it's quite chunky, that's okay, too). Spread the olive mixture evenly over swordfish steaks. Place in oven approximately 4-6" from top broiler flame. Broil 10-15 minutes or so – do not turn over. After 10 minutes, test with a fork to make sure fish is cooked through. It should be slightly pink in the center.

Shrimp in Thai Curry Paste

This is also good made with squid or a combo of shrimp, squid and scallops.

· SERVES 4 ·

2 cups jasmine rice
3½ cups water
2 Tbsp. peanut oil
3 large cloves garlic, pressed
2 Tbsp. red curry paste
2 lbs. large shrimp, peeled
3 Tbsp. palm sugar or honey
2 Tbsp. fish sauce or tamari
1 19-oz. can unsweetened coconut milk
4 Tbsp. chopped fresh cilantro

Rinse rice well & drain. Put into pot ∽ add 3½ cups water. Cover & bring to a boil. Reduce heat to low & simmer for 15 minutes. Remove from heat & let sit.

While the rice is cooking, heat oil in a wok or skillet ∽ add garlic & curry paste. Mix and cook for 1 minute. Add shrimp and stir-fry for 3 minutes. Add palm sugar, fish sauce, coconut milk and 3 Tbsp. cilantro. Cook, uncovered, for 10 minutes. Spoon over rice. Garnish with remaining cilantro.

Judy's Grilled Salmon with Spicy Sweet and Sour Marinade

Judy is one of those people who does a lot of things well and makes them look easy...!

· SERVES 4 ·

3 Tbsp. olive or canola oil
3 Tbsp. honey
½ cup orange juice
2 cloves garlic, pressed
1½ Tbsp. Dijon mustard
¼ tsp. Tabasco sauce
¼ tsp. hot red pepper flakes
¼ tsp. cayenne pepper
4 drops liquid smoke (look for at market)
2 Tbsp. fresh dill, finely chopped
2 lbs. salmon fillets

Mix all of the above ingredients (except for salmon) into a small pot. Heat on low for 5 minutes, stirring constantly. Remove from heat & allow to cool 10 minutes. Place salmon fillets onto a dish & pour ⅔ of marinade over fish & place in fridge to marinate for 1 hour. Prepare the grill... remove fish from fridge & let sit at room temperature while grill is heating up. Grill fish on oiled grate for about 7 minutes per side. Just as the fish is ready to come off the grill, heat remaining ⅓ of marinade in pot. Place fish onto a platter ~ pour hot marinade over top and serve.

Karen's Snapper Veracruzana

Serve with rice, avocado slices and a green salad.

· SERVES 4 ·

¼ cup olive oil
1 medium onion, chopped
2 large cloves garlic, pressed
1 carrot, julienned
¼ cup dry white wine
1 2-lb. can tomatoes, chopped
2 Tbsp. capers
15 small pimento-stuffed green olives, halved
2 fresh jalapeno peppers – cored, seeded & chopped
1 tsp. dried oregano
salt & pepper to taste
2 lbs. snapper fillets

Preheat oven to 350°. Heat olive oil in a skillet. Add onion, garlic and carrot – sauté 5 minutes. Add wine, tomatoes, capers, olives, jalapeno peppers, oregano, and salt & pepper to taste. Mix well and simmer on low heat for 10 minutes. Lightly oil a baking pan – place snapper fillets into pan and pour sauce over fish. Bake uncovered at 350° for 10-15 minutes. Fish should be flaky and moist.

Orange Roughy in a Yogurt Chive Sauce

Quick...Quick...Quick — the word for the 90's. Here's another quick & tasty fish dish. If orange roughy is not available, any mild white fish will do.

· SERVES 4 ·

2 lbs. orange roughy fillets
juice of 1 lemon
½ cup plain low-fat yogurt
¼ cup mayonnaise
3 Tbsp. fresh chives, chopped
paprika

Place fish onto a broiling pan and squeeze lemon over top. Mix yogurt, mayonnaise & chives together in a bowl. Spread evenly over fish & sprinkle with a little paprika.

Place in oven approximately 6" from top broiler and broil 10 minutes, or till fish flakes when tested with a fork.

Thai Grilled Squid

There is no middle ground with squid — you either love it or hate it.
If it gives you the willies, then try the marinade on boneless
chicken breasts, shrimp, scallops, tuna, swordfish, tofu...
Serve with Jasmine Rice and Stir-fried Snow Peas.

· SERVES 4 ·

2 lbs. cleaned squid
MARINADE:
juice of 1 lime
juice of 1 lemon
1 Tbsp. red curry paste
2 Tbsp. canola oil
2 Tbsp. fish sauce
2 Tbsp. chopped fresh cilantro
2 cloves garlic, pressed

Mix marinade ingredients together in a bowl. Place
squid in another bowl — pour marinade over squid.
Mix well and refrigerate 1 to 2 hours.
Remove squid from fridge. Mix well and let sit at
room temperature while you prepare the grill. Place
squid in an oiled fish basket made for grilling. Grill
squid on one side for about 7 to 10 minutes, then
flip and grill on the other side for 7 to 10 minutes.
Remove from grill and cut into rings... leave ten-
tacles whole ... and serve.

Shrimp Scampi over Angel Hair Pasta

Years ago I used butter when making Scampi — the fool that I was! Now I only use olive oil, so as not to clog our little arteries. It is every bit as good.

· SERVES 4 ·

1 lb. angel hair pasta (cappelletti)
1½ lbs. large uncooked shrimp, peeled & deveined
¼ cup extra-virgin olive oil
¼ cup dry sherry or white wine
6 large cloves garlic, pressed
juice of 2 lemons
2 Tbsp. freshly chopped parsley
salt & pepper to taste
½ cup freshly grated Parmesan cheese

Put up a large pot of water to boil for pasta. Meanwhile, place shrimp into a broiling pan & add all the remaining ingredients except for the cheese (and pasta, of course!). Mix well & place under broiler for about 5 minutes, then turn as well as you can by mixing with a wooden spoon. Broil for another 5 minutes. Pasta should be about done, as the angel hair cooks in virtually 2-3 minutes, & fresh pasta cooks even faster, so be sure not to overcook. Drain pasta and place into a large serving bowl. Spoon shrimp and sauce over pasta. Add cheese and toss well. Serve immediately.

Breaded Flounder

This is a recipe almost too ordinary to mention. However, it is delicious, takes virtually minutes to prepare,
and is a hit with kids and adults alike. It's best
served with buttered noodles, frozen petite peas and a
green salad for a comforting all-American meal.

· SERVES 4 ·

2 lbs. flounder fillets
juice of 2 lemons
1½ cup seasoned bread crumbs
olive oil

IMPORTANT NOTE: Have all other dishes prepared before cooking the flounder, as it takes
only a few minutes to cook. If there is a de-
lay, then place the cooked flounder in a warm
oven until ready to serve.

Place flounder fillets in a large bowl & squeeze
lemon over top. Place bread crumbs in another
bowl or plate. Put a fillet in crumbs & coat well.
Remove & set aside. Continue breading the remaining fillets. Heat a little olive oil in a large
skillet — place as many fillets as possible in
skillet to cook without crowding them. Cook
on medium heat for 3 minutes, then flip over
& cook another 3 minutes. Remove from skillet
& cover to keep warm while cooking the remaining
fillets.

Grilled Salmon

2 lbs. fresh salmon fillets

~ <u>MARINADE INGREDIENTS</u> ~

juice of 1 lemon
1 Tbsp. roasted sesame oil
1 Tbsp. tamari
3 Tbsp. hoison sauce
1 Tbsp. mirin
1 Tbsp. freshly grated ginger

Place fillets into a vessel for marinating. Mix marinade ingredients together in a bowl — pour over fish. Refrigerate one hour or longer. Remove from fridge and let stand at room temperature while you prepare the grill.
Place fish, skin side down, on hot grill. Grill for 5-7 minutes. Do not flip. Check with a fork ... salmon should be pink, not red when finished. Do n<u>ot</u> overcook.

Scallops with Mushrooms, Sun-Dried Tomatoes & Capers

A scrumptious, quick meal for all you guys & gals on the go!

· SERVES 2-4 ·

1 cup uncooked rice
1 lb. bay scallops
juice of 1 lemon
2 Tbsp. olive oil
½ lb. fresh mushrooms, sliced
7 sun-dried tomatoes, packed in oil (drain and cut into strips)
¼ cup dry sherry or white wine
2 large cloves garlic, pressed
1 Tbsp. dried parsley
3 Tbsp. capers
salt & pepper to taste

Cook rice as directed. Put scallops into a large bowl — add the remaining ingredients and mix well. Transfer to a broiling pan. Broil in oven about 4 to 6 inches from top broiler flame for 10 minutes. Remove from broiler. Serve over rice.

Swordfish in a Light Ginger Marinade

Simplicity ... the best way to prepare fish!

·SERVES 4·

2 lbs. swordfish steaks

<u>Marinade</u>:
juice of 1 large lemon
1 Tbsp. freshly grated ginger
2 Tbsp. roasted sesame oil
3 Tbsp. tamari or soy sauce
1 Tbsp. mirin — optional
1 small garlic clove, pressed

Place fish in a bowl, broiling pan, or whatever you have for marinating.

Make marinade by simply mixing all the ingredients together — pour over fish and marinate 2-3 hours in refrigerator, turning fish every hour.

Either broil or grill the fish, allowing 7-10 minutes on each side. Brush with marinade as needed.

The fish should flake with fork when done — do not overcook!

Salmon Fennel Cakes

Salmon and fennel pair up well in these special little fish cakes. A green salad with a balsamic vinaigrette complements them well.

· MAKES 8 GOOD-SIZE CAKES - SERVES 4 ·

1 lb. fresh salmon fillets
7 cups water
1 Tbsp. olive oil
¼ cup sherry
6 slices oat bread, broken into pieces
juice of 2 lemons
¼ cup onion, finely chopped
½ cup fennel, finely chopped (use stalks & feathery fronds)
3 Tbsp. Worcestershire sauce
3 Tbsp. Dijon mustard
1 egg, beaten
salt & pepper
olive oil

Poach salmon earlier in the day to allow it to cool. To poach ... bring 7 cups of water, 1 Tbsp. olive oil & ¼ cup sherry to a boil in a pan large enough to hold the salmon, but small enough so that the water will completely cover the fillets. When the water comes to a boil, put the fillets (skin side down) in and simmer on a low heat for 5 minutes or so until salmon is cooked. Test by piercing the thickest part of the fish with a fork. The fish should be flaky — do not overcook. Remove fish from pan and set aside to cool.

Flake the fish and place into a bowl with the bread pieces — mix. Add remaining ingredients except for the olive oil, and mix well with a wooden spoon or hands. Form into eight cakes.

Heat enough olive oil in a skillet to coat bottom. Place as many cakes as will fit without crowding. Cook on a medium heat for 5 minutes or so, or until nice & brown — then flip and brown on the other side.

Cover to keep warm while cooking the remaining cakes.

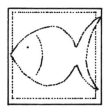 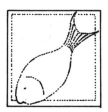  

Grilled Salmon with Tomato Cilantro Sauce

Que Rico!

· SERVES 4 ·

2 Tbsp. olive oil
1 large clove garlic, pressed
1 small onion, chopped
½ red bell pepper, chopped
1 pasilla chili pepper ~ optional
1 cup fresh cilantro, chopped
8 plum tomatoes, chopped
juice of 2 limes
salt to taste

2 lbs. salmon fillets
juice of 1 lime
1 Tbsp. olive oil

Prepare grill... meanwhile, start sauce by heating 2 Tbsp. olive oil in a skillet. Add garlic & onion ~ sauté 3 minutes. Add both peppers ~ sauté 5 minutes. Add cilantro, tomatoes, lime juice & a little salt. Mix ~ cover ~ simmer on low for 20 minutes, mixing often. As sauce is simmering, place salmon fillets on a plate & squeeze lime over top. Drizzle with 1 Tbsp. olive oil. Grill fish for about 5 minutes per side... check with fork to see if cooked ~ do not overcook. Place fillets on a large serving platter ~ spoon sauce over top & garnish with a little fresh chopped cilantro. Serve with rice and sliced avocado.

Poultry

Thai Chicken Curry

Very delicious yet easy to make ~ what more can you ask for ?!

· SERVES 4-6 ·

2 cups jasmine rice
2 Tbsp. peanut oil
3 large cloves garlic, pressed
1 tsp. freshly grated ginger
2 Tbsp. red curry paste
2 lbs. boneless chicken breasts, cut into bite-size pieces
juice of 1 lime
¼ cup Thai basil, chopped ~ optional
2 Tbsp. fish sauce or tamari
1 14-oz. can unsweetened coconut milk
½ cup water

Begin cooking rice as directed. While rice is cooking, heat oil in a wok or skillet & add garlic, ginger & curry paste. Stir-fry for 1 minute. Add chicken, lime juice & Thai basil. Stir-fry 7 minutes. Add fish sauce, coconut milk & water. Stir-fry 10 minutes.

Serve over rice.

Apple – Orange Roasted Chicken

Another delightful way to roast chicken. Apples are placed into cavity to be later mashed into the pan juices. I also like to place carrots and yams around the chicken, so that most of your dinner is cooked together in one large pan – a part of the "no fuss - no muss" principle.

· SERVES 4-6 ·

1 6-lb. whole roasting chicken
salt & pepper
2 apples, peeled & quartered
1 cup orange juice
½ cup dry sherry or white or red wine
4 Tbsp. olive oil
4 yams, peeled & quartered
6 carrots, peeled & cut into thirds
paprika

Preheat oven to 325°. Rinse chicken under cold water to clean. Place in a large roasting pan with lid. Sprinkle cavity with salt & pepper. Place apple quarters inside of cavity. Pour orange juice, wine and olive oil over chicken, and sprinkle generously with salt & pepper. Arrange yams and carrots around chicken (try not to crowd the chicken, so that it can brown nicely). Sprinkle paprika over chicken.

Cover and bake at 325° for 45 minutes, basting both chicken and veggies every 15 minutes. Uncover and bake 1½ hours, basting everything every 20 minutes. When chicken is done, remove from oven ⌐ cover and let sit 10 minutes before carving.

When ready to carve, remove carrots and yams, and place in a serving dish. Cover to keep hot.

Place chicken on a cutting board and carve. Remove apples from cavity and mash into pan juices with a potato masher.

Place chicken on a serving platter and spoon pan juices over top. Serve.

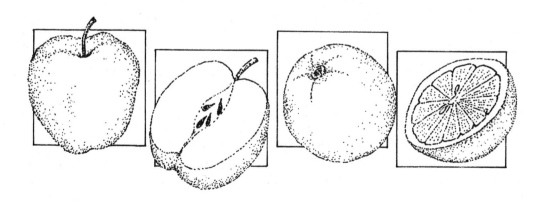

Chicken Biriyani

We realize that this is a long and scary list of ingredients, but it all goes into one pot, and the preparation is quite simple. It is well worth the effort...!

· SERVES 4-6 ·

1½ cups uncooked brown or white Basmati rice

¼ cup safflower oil

1 large yellow onion, chopped

6 large cloves garlic, pressed

2 Tbsp. freshly grated ginger

1 3-4 lb. chicken, cut into pieces (remove skin)

1 Tbsp. cumin seed or ground cumin

* 1 tsp. ground cinnamon

* 1 tsp. ground cardamom

* 1 tsp. whole mustard seed

3 Tbsp. curry powder (use good quality)

* 1 tsp. grated orange peel

* ½ tsp. ground cloves

* ½ tsp. ground nutmeg

½ cup fresh cilantro, chopped

salt to taste

juice of 1 lemon

juice of 1 orange

1 cup raisins

3 cups water

1 cup frozen peas

1 cup plain yogurt

Cook rice as directed. Set aside. In a large heavy-bottom pot with lid, heat oil. Add onion, garlic & ginger ‿ sauté 5 minutes. Add chicken pieces & brown for 5 minutes on each side. Remove chicken ‿ add spices & remaining ingredients, except for the last three. Sauté 5 minutes. Return chicken to pot ‿ add water & cover. Cook on low heat for 1 hour, stirring often. Add peas & yogurt ‿ cover & let simmer 15 minutes. Serve over rice.

* IF YOU ARE MISSING A FEW OF THESE INGREDIENTS, DON'T WORRY ABOUT IT, AS IT WILL BE GREAT ANYWAY!

Lemon Roasted Chicken

... my favorite way to roast chicken

· SERVES 4-6 ·

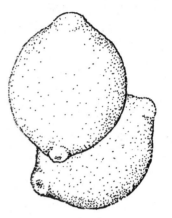

1 6-lb. whole roasting chicken
2 Tbsp. olive oil
juice of 2 lemons
2 cloves garlic, cut into halves
½ cup dry white or red wine
1 Tbsp. fresh rosemary, chopped
1 Tbsp. fresh thyme, chopped
salt & pepper

Preheat oven to 350°. Rinse chicken under cold water and pat dry with paper towel. Sprinkle some salt & pepper into the cavity. Place chicken in a roasting pan, and drizzle olive oil over top. Squeeze lemons over chicken, then put the lemon rinds plus the garlic halves into the cavity. Pour wine over chicken. Sprinkle liberally with salt and pepper, and sprinkle herbs over top.

Place chicken in oven and roast uncovered at 350° for 2 hours. Baste often with pan juices. If juices diminish, add some wine or water to bottom of pan. When done, remove from oven, cover, and let sit 7 minutes before carving. Carve and place on a serving platter, spoon some juices from pan over top and serve.

Grilled Curried Chicken

Although grilling imparts a wonderful flavor to chicken, if you can't or wish not to grill, then broiling would work as well.
Serve with Basmati Rice, Cucumber Raita & Steamed Broccoli.

· SERVES 4-6 ·

3 whole boneless chicken breasts, cut into
6 halves
1 cup plain yogurt
a one-inch piece of fresh ginger
1 large clove garlic, peeled
2 Tbsp. curry powder
1 Tbsp. cumin powder
juice of 1 lemon
1 tsp. salt

Rinse chicken under cold water. Pat dry with a paper towel. Place in a bowl or container to marinate. Place all remaining ingredients in a food processor or blender, and purée. Pour over chicken ~ mix to cover completely.

Refrigerate several hours or overnight, turning the chicken a few times. Remove chicken from refrigerator & let sit at room temperature while you prepare the grill. Grill 7 to 10 minutes per side. Baste often with marinade.

Sesame Chicken

You probably thought that this was going to be an exotic Asian recipe. But no — it's just an all-American family favorite. Try it... it's simple... Kids love it, and the sesame seeds are loaded with calcium.

· SERVES 4-6 ·

8 chicken breast halves (4 whole)
juice of 1 large lemon
2 cups seasoned bread crumbs
$\frac{1}{2}$ cup sesame seeds
1 tsp. salt

Preheat oven to 350°. Oil a large baking pan. Remove skin from chicken and discard. Rinse chicken under cold water and pat dry with a paper towel. Place in a large bowl. Squeeze lemon over top.

Place bread crumbs, sesame seeds and salt into another large bowl and mix well.

Place one piece of chicken in bread crumbs and coat well. Remove from bowl and place in a baking dish.

Repeat with remaining chicken.

Bake uncovered at 350° for 1 hour.

Thai Roast Duck

A few Thai ingredients make for a delicious roast duck. Since duck tends to be fatty, cook it on a rack — or remove the fat with a baster as it cooks.

· SERVES 4 ·

1 5-lb. duck
1 tsp. salt
1 tsp. red curry paste
2 cloves garlic, pressed
1 tsp. roasted sesame oil
1 Tbsp. freshly grated ginger
2 Tbsp. tamari
2 Tbsp. honey
juice of 1 lemon

Rinse duck under cold water — remove & discard any excess fat. Mix salt, curry paste & garlic together in a little bowl. Rub evenly over duck & place duck onto a rack in a roasting pan. Place in preheated 350° oven & bake uncovered for 1 hour (remove fat that accumulates on bottom of pan with a baster frequently, if not using a rack). After 1 hour of cooking, mix sesame oil, ginger, tamari, honey & lemon juice together in a bowl — pour over duck. Bake 1 hour, basting every 15 minutes (most of excess fat should have been removed in the 1st hour of cooking). Remove from oven. Cover and let sit 10 minutes before carving.

Chicken with Arugula & Capers Over Wild Rice

Arugula, or rocket, is best known for the bite it adds to a salad; however, the greens are delicious cooked as well.

·SERVES 4·

2 cups wild rice
3 Tbsp. olive oil
5 large cloves garlic, pressed
1 large bunch fresh arugula, washed & chopped
1 tsp. dried basil
2 lbs. boneless chicken breasts, cut in bite-size pieces
3 large ripe tomatoes, chopped, or 1 lb. canned tomatoes
2 heaping Tbsp. capers
½ cup dry white wine
salt & pepper to taste

Begin cooking rice as directed. Heat olive oil in a large skillet. Add garlic, arugula & basil — sauté 5 minutes. Add chicken and sauté 5 more minutes. Add tomatoes, capers, wine, salt & pepper. Cover and cook on medium heat for 20 minutes, stirring occasionally.
Serve over rice.

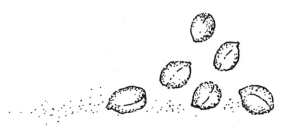

Indian Roast Chicken

〜 memorable served with Three Bean Dal, basmati rice, steamed broccoli and Cucumber Raita.

• SERVES 4 •

1 3-4 lb. chicken, split in half (important)
juice of 2 oranges or ½ cup O.J.
juice of 1 lemon
salt & pepper
1 tsp. fennel seed
1 tsp. cumin seed
1 tsp. coriander seed
1 tsp. mustard seed
1 large clove garlic, pressed
2 Tbsp. freshly grated ginger
2 Tbsp. fresh chopped cilantro

Rinse chicken under cold water 〜 leave skin intact. Place in a large bowl or container. Add orange and lemon juice 〜 sprinkle generously with salt & pepper, and set aside while you toast the seeds.

Put all the seeds into a dry skillet & toast on a medium heat until fragrant... about 5-7 minutes. Remove from pan and grind either in a mortar and pestle, or in an electric coffee grinder (God bless those little modern inventions!).

Put ground seeds in a bowl — add garlic and ginger — mix well. Smear over chicken, and refrigerate the chicken for at least two hours.

When ready to cook, remove chicken from the fridge and let sit 10 minutes while you preheat oven to 350°.

Oil a baking pan and place chicken halves in pan, skin side up. Pour any additional marinade over chicken.

Bake at 350° for 1½ hours, basting often.

Remove from oven — cut into pieces — spoon pan juices over top — sprinkle with chopped cilantro and serve.

Thai Chicken Satay

Grilled chicken on skewers with a slightly spicy peanut sauce for dipping — serve as an appetizer or main course with jasmine rice, Thai Cucumber Salad and Stir-Fry Snow Peas.

· SERVES 4-6 ·

2½ lbs. boneless chicken breasts, cut into thin strips

MARINADE:

juice of 1 lemon
juice of 1 lime
2 Tbsp. chopped cilantro
2 Tbsp. peanut oil
1 Tbsp. freshly grated ginger
2 cloves garlic, pressed
1 Tbsp. fish sauce
1 Tbsp. tamari

Mix all the marinade ingredients together in a bowl — place chicken into a large bowl and pour marinade over top. Mix well — cover and refrigerate for at least 2 hours. Remove the chicken from the fridge as you prepare the grill. Also, make the Satay Sauce (recipe follows) while the grill is heating up.

Soak approximately 10 wooden skewers in water, or use metal skewers if you have them, and forget about soaking. Thread chicken pieces onto skewers and set aside.

When the grill is hot, place skewers on oiled grill and cook chicken for 8 minutes on one side. Baste with the extra marinade, then flip and grill for 8 more minutes. Check to see if chicken is done... you may need to flip over and repeat 5 more minutes per side, depending on how tightly the skewers are threaded & how large the chicken pieces are. Serve with Satay Sauce.

Satay Sauce

2 Tbsp. peanut oil
2 Tbsp. freshly chopped onion
2 cloves garlic, pressed
1 Tbsp. freshly grated ginger
1 tsp. red curry paste
2 Tbsp. fish sauce
3 Tbsp. sugar
juice of 1 lemon
2 Tbsp. tamari
1 14-oz. can of unsweetened coconut milk
4 heaping Tbsp. smooth peanut butter

Heat oil in a skillet ~ add onion, garlic & ginger ~ sauté on low for 7 minutes. Add remaining 7 ingredients & mix well till nice and smooth. Cook on a low heat till hot... approximately 7 minutes, stirring often. Serve on the side as a dipping sauce for the grilled chicken.

Asian Grilled Chicken

For the best results the chicken should marinate overnight in the fridge, but if that is not possible, then at least for several hours.

· SERVES 4-8 ·

4 whole boneless chicken breasts, cut into halves
MARINADE:
¼ cup hoison sauce
¼ cup dry sherry
¼ cup tamari
3 Tbsp. roasted sesame oil
¼ cup rice vinegar
3 Tbsp. mirin
2 Tbsp. freshly grated ginger
1 large clove garlic, pressed
juice of 1 lemon
1 Tbsp. chili oil
3 Tbsp. fresh chopped cilantro

*SERVE WITH RICE AND GRILLED VEGETABLES

Rinse chicken under cold water & pat dry with a paper towel. Place chicken in a large bowl or container for marinating. Mix all of the marinade ingredients together well, and pour over chicken. Marinate in fridge as long as possible. Remove chicken from fridge & let sit at room temperature while you prepare the grill. Grill 7 to 10 minutes on each side, brushing often with marinade. *

Myra's Turkey Patties

Serve these flavorful patties with mashed potatoes and fried onions, or on a bun with melted cheese, fried onions & the works.

· SERVES 4 (MAKES 8 PATTIES) ·

1½ lbs. ground turkey
1 large egg, beaten
½ cup finely chopped onion
2 cloves garlic, pressed
2 Tbsp. dried parsley ⎫
2 Tbsp. dried dill   ⎬ and/or
2 Tbsp. Worcestershire sauce
½ cup seasoned bread crumbs
salt & pepper
olive oil for frying

Place the turkey in a large bowl ~ add egg & mix well. Add remaining ingredients except for the oil. Mix well. Form into 8 patties. Heat enough olive oil in a skillet to cover bottom of pan. Place patties in pan & cook on a medium heat for 10 minutes, or till nice and brown. Flip and repeat on other side. If you can't fit all the patties into the skillet at one time, then keep cooked patties warm by covering, while you cook the rest.

NOTE: THESE PATTIES CAN BE BROILED IF YOU PREFER ...

Roast Stuffed Chicken

Yummers!

· SERVES 4-6 ·

Stuffing:

1 cup broth, vegetable or chicken
1 loaf of oat bread, broken up
3 Tbsp. butter, melted
1 small onion, chopped
3 stalks celery, chopped
2 Tbsp. freshly chopped parsley
3 Tbsp. dry sherry or white wine
salt & pepper to taste

Chicken:

1 5-6 lb. whole roasting chicken
$\frac{1}{2}$ cup orange juice
$\frac{1}{4}$ cup sherry or dry white wine
salt & pepper to taste

Remove giblets from chicken, rinse and put in a pot with 3 cups water. Cover and bring to a boil. Simmer for $\frac{1}{2}$ hour. This is to make broth, so, if using vegetable broth, just dissolve a veggie bouillon cube in water – and toss the giblets. Rinse the chicken in cold water and set aside.

To make stuffing, break bread into pieces in a large bowl and set aside. In a large skillet, melt butter ~ add onion, celery and parsley. Sauté 5 minutes. Add wine, cover and simmer 5 minutes. Spoon skillet contents into the bowl of bread and mix well. Ladle 1 cup of broth over bread & veggies. Mix well. Season to taste with salt & pepper. Stuff into chicken cavity. Place chicken in a roasting pan. Pour orange juice & wine over chicken. Sprinkle liberally with salt & pepper. Preheat oven to 350°.

Bake, covered, for 45 minutes in a 350° oven. Baste every 20 minutes. Reduce heat & bake uncovered at 350° for another 1½ hours. Continue to baste every 20 minutes. To know if chicken is done, pierce thigh with a fork~ juices should be clear, not pink.

Carve chicken and place on a platter. Spoon stuffing in a bowl. Spoon some of the pan juices over chicken and serve.

Stir-fry Chicken with Thai Basil and Hot Pepper

Surprisingly easy and quick to make – a winner!

· SERVES 4 ·

2 cups uncooked jasmine or basmati rice
3 Tbsp. peanut oil
7 large cloves garlic, pressed
1 cup chopped Thai basil
¼ cup chopped cilantro
2 lbs. boneless chicken breasts, cut into bite-size pieces
1 Thai pepper or ½ tsp. hot pepper flakes
4 Tbsp. fish sauce or tamari

Cook rice as directed.

Meanwhile, heat oil in a wok or large skillet. Add garlic, Thai basil and cilantro. Stir-fry 1 minute. Add chicken and hot pepper. Stir-fry 10 minutes. Add fish sauce or tamari. Stir-fry 1 minute.

Serve over rice.

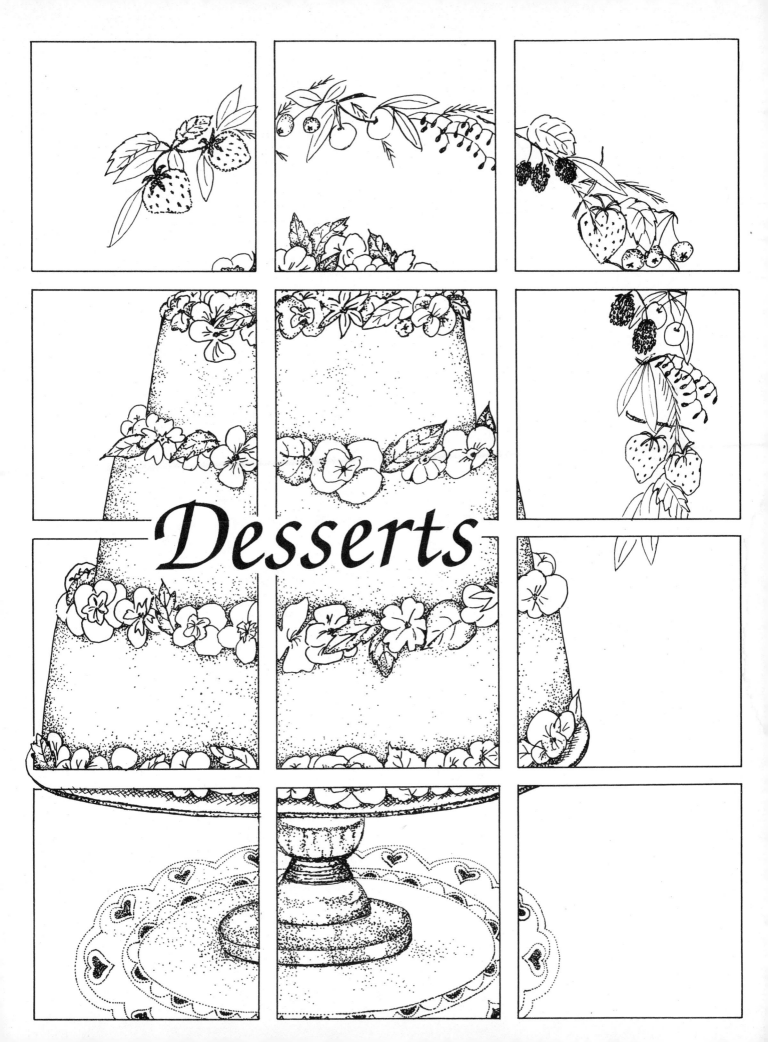

Desserts

Penny's Peachberry Pie

— our friend Penny ... quite the baker!

Pie Crust (see page 217)

Fruit Filling:
   1½ cups fresh ripe peaches, peeled & sliced
   ½ cup raspberries
   2 cups plain yogurt
   1 cup sugar
   2 eggs, beaten
   1 tsp. vanilla
   1 tsp. cinnamon

Crumb Topping:
   4 Tbsp. butter
   ½ cup sugar
   1 tsp. cinnamon
   ¾ cup flour

Preheat oven to 350°. Make crust as directed. Mix all the filling ingredients together in a large bowl & set aside. To make topping, melt butter in a small pot — add sugar and cinnamon. Mix well & add flour. Mix with a fork till crumbly — set aside. Pour filling ingredients into pie crust & sprinkle crumb topping evenly over filling. Place pie pan onto a cookie sheet and bake at 350° for 50 minutes. Cool to room temperature and serve. ♡♡♡

Baked Apples

Warm... comforting... somewhat dietetic ⌐ that's if you don't top it with a ton of vanilla ice cream!

· SERVES 4-6 ·

8-10 large apples ⌐ leave peels on & cut into quarters (McIntosh or Cortland)

2 Tbsp. butter

½ cup pure maple syrup

1 tsp. cinnamon

juice of 1 orange

Preheat oven to 325°. Butter an 11x14" baking pan. Place apples into pan.

Melt butter in a small pot ⌐ add maple syrup, cinnamon and orange juice. Mix well & pour over apples.

Bake, uncovered, for 45 minutes at 325° ⌐ basting often with juices. Serve warm.

Lynn's Cheesecake

Lynnie... another great cook! This incredible dessert should be refrigerated overnight, so plan accordingly. ♡ ♡ ♡ ♡ ♡ ♡

CRUST:
¼ cup butter
1¼ cups graham cracker crumbs
¼ cup sugar

SOUR CREAM TOPPING:
2 cups sour cream
2 tsp. vanilla
¼ cup sugar

CREAM CHEESE FILLING:
3 8-oz. pkgs. cream cheese
1½ cups sugar
4 eggs
1 tsp. vanilla

Butter a 10" spring-form cake pan. Make crust by melting butter in a small pot — add sugar & graham cracker crumbs. Mix well. Press into buttered pan... press along sides but not all the way up. Chill while you make filling.

Preheat oven to 350°. Mix cream cheese with sugar & beat till fluffy. Add eggs one at a time, beating after each addition. Beat in vanilla — pour into pan. Bake at 350° for 50 minutes. Remove from oven — let sit 15 minutes — and reset oven temperature to 450°. Make topping by combining sour cream, vanilla & sugar together in a bowl. Mix well. Spread over cake & bake at 450° for 10 minutes.

Remove from oven & cool to room temperature, then chill overnight. Remove from pan before serving.

Mimsy's Mango Upside-Down Cake

 a true Hawaiian delight

· MAKES AN 8" CAKE ·

2 cups sliced ripe mangoes (2 large mangoes)
2 Tbsp. lime or lemon juice
1 Tbsp. butter
⅓ cup light brown sugar
1¼ cups flour
2 tsp. baking powder
¼ tsp. salt

¼ cup sugar
¼ cup butter
1 egg, beaten
½ cup milk

Preheat oven to 375° and butter an 8" cake pan. Place sliced mangoes into a bowl — add lime or lemon juice & mix well. Set aside as you melt 1 Tbsp. butter in a small pot, on a low heat. Pour melted butter into bottom of buttered cake pan. Swirl to cover bottom and sprinkle brown sugar over the melted butter. Spread mango slices evenly over the brown sugar and set aside.

Mix flour, baking powder & salt together in a bowl & set aside. Beat sugar & butter together in a bowl. Add egg & beat. Add ½ dry ingredients & beat — add milk & beat. Add remaining dry ingredients & beat well. Pour batter over mangoes. Bake at 375° for 1 hour. Remove from oven & turn upside-down onto a platter. Serve warm.

Tapioca Pudding

What could be more comforting on a cold winter eve ... or more fattening, for that matter! Oh well, let's at least make it for the kids.

· SERVES 6-8 ·

1 cup small tapioca pearls
2 cups water
4 cups milk
¾ cup pure maple syrup
    or raw sugar

pinch of salt
1 tsp. vanilla
2 eggs, beaten
cinnamon

Place tapioca and water into a good-size pot. Cover & let sit 20 minutes. Add milk. Place pot on stove ~ cover and begin cooking on a very low heat, stirring often.

Beat eggs, maple syrup, salt and vanilla together in a bowl. Take out ½ cup of hot tapioca from pot and mix in with egg mixture. Return to pot. Stir well ~ cover & continue cooking on a low heat for about 30 minutes, stirring often to prevent sticking.

Remove from heat and pour into custard cups. Sprinkle a little cinnamon on each individual cup. Let cool to room temperature.

Refrigerate a couple of hours before serving, or if you prefer, serve it slightly warm or at room temperature.

Ginger Pear Crisp

The piquant flavor of ginger pairs well with the smooth subtleness of pears. Serve alone... warm ~ or topped with vanilla ice cream.

· SERVES 6-8 ·

8 pears – Anjou or Bartlett – cored & chopped
1 heaping Tbsp. freshly grated ginger
$\frac{1}{2}$ cup pure maple syrup or raw sugar
Juice of 1 orange

Topping:
8 Tbsp. butter (don't worry... it makes a big crisp)
$\frac{1}{2}$ cup maple syrup
1 cup unbleached flour
1 cup quick-cooking oats
$\frac{1}{2}$ cup chopped walnuts
1 tsp. cinnamon

Preheat oven to 350° & butter an 8 x 12" baking dish. Place pears, ginger, $\frac{1}{2}$ cup maple syrup & O.J. into a bowl. Mix well. Spoon into baking dish & set aside as you make topping.

Melt butter in a medium pot ~ add maple syrup & mix. Add flour, oats, walnuts & cinnamon. Mix well with a fork till crumbly. Sprinkle evenly over pears.

Bake at 350° for 45 minutes. Serve warm.

Applesauce

Applesauce is a non-fat dessert loved by all. In the fall when apples are so very abundant, I will make large batches at a time. It will keep in an air-tight container for weeks in the fridge, plus it freezes well... to be enjoyed at any time throughout the year.

• YIELDS 10-12 CUPS •

16 large McIntosh apples
  (peeled, cored & coarsely chopped)
3 cups water
1 cup honey
1 Tbsp. cinnamon

Place apples and water in a large pot. Cover and bring to a boil. Reduce heat to low and simmer for 30 minutes.

Stir with wooden spoon... apples should be soft, and turn into sauce by stirring. Add honey and cinnamon ~ mix well.

Allow to cool to room temperature ~ then chill before serving.

Ellen's Marble Pound Cake

~ as passed down from Ellen's mom

· MAKES A 10" TUBE PAN CAKE ·

3 cups sifted flour
2 tsp. baking powder
½ tsp. salt
1 cup butter
2 cups sugar
3 eggs, beaten

1 cup milk
1½ tsp. vanilla
¾ cup chocolate syrup
(it's easy & it works!)
¼ tsp. baking soda

Preheat oven to 350° and butter a 10" tube pan. Mix flour, baking powder and salt together in a bowl. Set aside.

Cream butter and sugar well. Add eggs & mix well. Add vanilla to milk. Add ⅓ cup milk mixture to butter mixture & beat. Add ⅓ cup dry ingredients & beat. Repeat with ⅓ milk - ⅓ dry - ⅓ milk - ⅓ dry & beat well. Spoon two thirds of batter into buttered cake pan. Mix chocolate syrup with baking soda & add to remaining batter. Mix well. Pour into cake pan ~ do not mix.

Bake at 350° for 70 minutes. Remove from oven.

Let cake sit 1 hour before removing from pan ~ then allow to cool to room temperature.

Patti's Ricotta Cheese Pie

Patti says that when she makes this pie in the summer when Bing cherries are in season, she adds about 18 cherries ... pitted & cut in half ... to the filling before baking.

· MAKES 1 LOVELY 10" DEEP-DISH PIE ·

CRUST:
2 cups flour
¼ tsp. salt
½ cup butter, cut into
     small pieces
2 Tbsp. brandy or
     cognac

FILLING:
3 Tbsp. toasted pine nuts
2 Tbsp. chopped almonds
4 eggs
1 cup sugar
1½ tsp. vanilla
1½ lbs. ricotta cheese

Preheat oven to 375°. Make crust by placing flour & salt into a large bowl or food processor ~ add butter and mix well. Add brandy or cognac, and mix till the dough holds together. Roll out & place into a 10" rectangular Pyrex dish or baking dish with sides. Flute edges & set aside. To make filling ... place pine nuts in a dry skillet and toast till golden on low heat (takes only a minute or two). Remove from pan & mix with chopped almonds. Set aside. Place eggs in a mixing bowl & beat well. Gradually add sugar as you beat. Add vanilla & beat. Add ricotta cheese, pine nuts & almonds. Beat well. Spoon into pie crust & bake at 375° for 40 minutes. Allow to cool and serve at room temperature.

Fanny's Kugel

This incredible kugel appeared in our first book, _The Not-Strictly Vegetarian Cookbook_... however, Fanny insisted upon making a few changes. If you didn't already know, a kugel is a noodle pudding... and this is by far the best ever!

· SERVES 6-8 ·

FILLING :
8 oz. fine egg noodles
4 eggs
1 cup sugar
2 cups milk
4 oz. evaporated milk
¾ lb. cream cheese
1 Tbsp. vanilla

TOPPING :
4 Tbsp. butter
2 Tbsp. sugar
1 Tbsp. cinnamon
8 graham crackers, crushed

Preheat oven to 350°. Butter a large 9 x 13" baking pan. Cook noodles as directed. Whilst the noodles are cooking, place all the remaining filling ingredients in a large bowl & beat well with an electric mixer. Drain noodles in a colander. Mix noodles into the filling ingredients with a wooden spoon. Pour into buttered baking dish. Set aside while you make topping.
Melt butter in a small pot ~ add sugar & cinnamon ~ mix well. Add crushed graham crackers & mix well. Sprinkle topping evenly over noodle mixture. Bake at 350° for 45 minutes.

Joan's Gingered Rhubarb Pie

· SERVES 6 ·

1 pie crust (see pg. 217)

4 cups chopped fresh rhubarb
¼ cup water
¼ cup fresh ginger, peeled & minced
⅓ cup fresh mint, chopped
⅔ cup honey

Make pie crust as directed, and set aside while you make the filling.

Simmer all the above ingredients together (except for the pie crust of course... not that I needed to mention that...!) in a large pot for 15 minutes, stirring often.

Pour filling into pie crust and bake at 350° for 35 minutes.

Serve warm or at room temperature... and we think that vanilla ice cream would make it even more divine!

Brownies

I usually double the recipe when making these scrumptious brownies.

· MAKES 1 DOZEN ·

¼ lb. lightly salted butter
6 oz. milk chocolate chips
2 eggs
1 tsp. vanilla
½ cup raw sugar (white will do)
½ cup unbleached flour
½ cup coarsely chopped walnuts

Preheat oven to 350° ~ butter a 9" square baking pan and set aside.

Place butter and chocolate chips into a small saucepan and melt on a low heat, stirring often. Remove from heat and allow to cool while you beat the eggs, vanilla and sugar in a mixing bowl. Add flour a little at a time, beating as you do. Add chocolate and butter, and mix well. Add nuts and mix in. Pour into pan.

Bake in middle of oven for 20 minutes, testing middle with a dry toothpick, which should come out clean when done.

Remove from oven ~ allow to cool ~ cut into squares.

Our Favorite Pie Crust

• FOR A ONE-CRUST 9" PIE PAN

6 Tbsp. butter

1 heaping cup flour (unbleached white, or ½ whole wheat pastry flour... or use all whole wheat pastry flour... but make sure it is pastry flour, as whole wheat bread flour is too heavy)

2-3 Tbsp. ice cold water

Blend butter and flour well with a pastry blender, fork, or in a food processor. It should look quite mealy. Add water a little at a time, as you continue to mix...until it all sticks together. Do not use too much water... it should stick, but should not be too sticky (does that make any sense?!). Roll out.

Apple / Pear Torte

~ Divine

<u>Pie Crust</u>: (see page 217)

<u>Apple / Pear Filling</u>:
3 large McIntosh or Winesap apples
~ cored, peeled & chopped
3 large pears ~
   Bartlett or Anjou...washed, cored & chopped (do not peel)
1 level Tbsp. cinnamon
¼ tsp. mace
¼ cup pure maple syrup or raw sugar

<u>Cream Filling</u>:
1 8-oz. pkg. cream cheese (feel free to substitute
                          "light" cream cheese)
1 large egg
¼ cup pure maple syrup or raw sugar
1 tsp. vanilla

Preheat oven to 350°. Make pie crust as directed on page 217. Roll out, place in a 9" or 10" pie plate, and flute edges. Set aside as you prepare the apples & pears.

To make apple / pear filling ~ simply place all the apple / pear ingredients in a bowl and mix well.

Set aside as you make the cream filling.

To make the cream filling — simply place the cream filling ingredients either in a bowl & mix with beaters, or put into a food processor and whirl till it's blended.

Spoon cream filling into pie crust, then spoon apple/pear mixture evenly on top.

Bake in a preheated oven for 50 to 60 minutes. Cool to room temperature before serving.

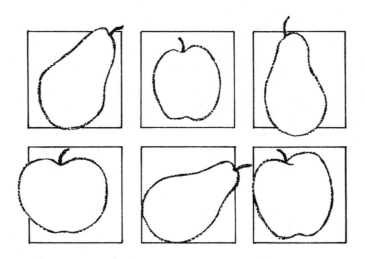

Kaya and Matthew's Chocolate Banana Chip Cake

Kaya and Matthew decided that they wanted to bake a cake for the book. They came up with some very wild and creative ideas, most sounding great in theory yet not really workable. This was the tamest of the lot. ♡ ♡ ♡

· MAKES A 10" TUBE PAN CAKE ·

12 oz. semi-sweet chocolate chips, crushed
½ lb. butter, softened
1 cup turbinado sugar
4 medium eggs
2 very ripe bananas
1 tsp. vanilla
3 cups unbleached white flour
3 tsp. baking powder
1 cup milk

Crush chocolate chips — a food processor does this job well... if you don't have one, then put the chips into a plastic bag and roll over them with a rolling pin.

Preheat oven to 350°.

Butter a tube-style cake pan. Place butter & sugar into a mixing bowl — beat until creamy.

Add eggs, bananas and vanilla – beat for 3 minutes.

Mix flour and baking powder together in another bowl. Add 1 cup of flour mixture to butter mixture and beat well. Add ⅓ cup milk and mix. Then add another cup of flour and beat well … then another ⅓ cup of milk. Mix and repeat with remaining flour and milk. Beat till well mixed. Add chocolate chips and mix well again.

Spoon batter into buttered cake pan and bake at 350° for 1 hour.

Remove from oven and allow to cool 1 hour before removing from pan.

Remove from pan, then let it sit a few hours until it's at room temperature. Kaya and Matthew think it best served with a large glass of cold milk!

Apple Crumb Pie

This pie is piled high with apples and a nut crumb topping. Serve warm with vanilla ice cream.

• MAKES ONE BIG BEAUTIFUL PIE •

<u>Crust</u> (see page 217)

<u>Filling</u>:
10 large McIntosh or Winesap apples — peeled, cored & chopped
1 Tbsp. cinnamon
¼ tsp. mace
juice of 1 orange
¾ cup turbinado or regular sugar

<u>Nut Crumb Topping</u>:
3 Tbsp. butter
½ cup turbinado or regular sugar
1 cup finely chopped walnuts
1 cup flour

Preheat oven to 325°.

Prepare crust as directed. Set aside.

Prepare apples ... place in a large bowl and add remaining filling ingredients. Mix well and set aside as you make topping.

Melt butter in a small pot — add sugar and mix. Add

walnuts & flour. Mix to make crumbs.

Spoon filling into pie crust. Now, to put the crumb topping on, I find it best to spoon it evenly over apples and pat gently with my hands to keep it from falling off.

Place pie pan on a cookie sheet (to prevent dripping on oven) and bake at 325° for 1 hour.

Serve warm or at room temperature.

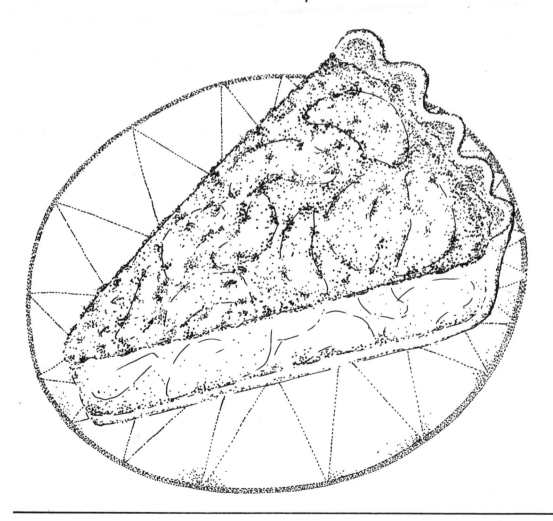

Wild Carrot Cake
With CREAM CHEESE ICING, Of Course!

The winter of 1994 was brutal... it was the 7th blizzard in two months... I was trapped inside... life was becoming one big maddening blur... Cooking & eating had become my life... I stumbled into the kitchen, passed out & when I finally came to, this cake was sitting on the counter! My family said that I made it and that it was one of my best. Somehow in my crazed state, I managed to scribble down the ingredients and directions. Who would dare to try it... ??

· MAKES ONE BIG WILD CAKE ·

2 cups unbleached white flour
3 tsp. baking powder
1 Tbsp. cinnamon
½ tsp. mace
1 cup turbinado sugar
3 eggs, beaten
1 cup canola oil
1 tsp. vanilla
3 cups grated carrots
16-oz. can crushed pineapple
1 cup chopped walnuts
1 cup raisins
1 cup unsweetened shredded coconut

Preheat oven to 325° and oil two 9" cake pans. Mix flour, baking powder, cinnamon, mace and sugar together in a large bowl. In another bowl beat eggs with oil and vanilla — add to the dry ingredients and mix well (I was told that I used a wooden spoon only). Add carrots, pineapple (liquid and all), walnuts, raisins & coconut. Mix well.

Spoon batter into the two oiled cake pans. Place in middle of oven and bake at 325° for 35 minutes. Remove from oven — allow to cool for ½ hour, then remove from pans. Let sit at room temperature 2 hours before icing. Cream Cheese Icing follows.....

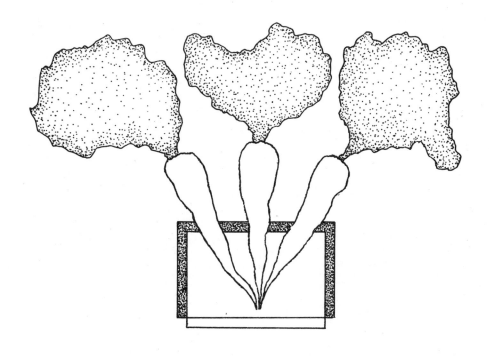

Cream Cheese Icing

~ makes enough to ice a big (wild!) carrot cake

8 oz. cream cheese
8 oz. sour cream
¼ cup maple syrup

Simply place all the ingredients into a bowl and beat with a mixer till smooth. Spread some on top of one layer, then place the other layer on top of that, and spread the remaining icing everywhere.

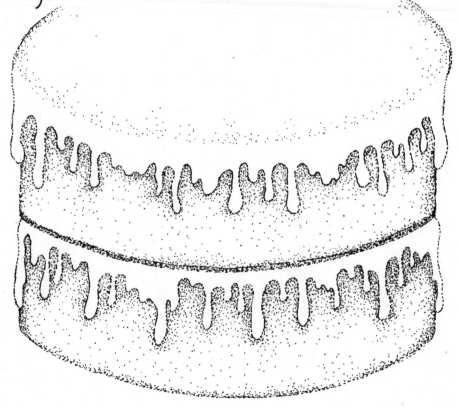

Cranberry Fruit Compote

Perfect served with a Thanksgiving dinner – or serve as a dessert alone, or topped with vanilla ice cream. Also wonderful with breakfast or brunch.

· SERVES 6-8 ·

1 cup dried mission figs
1 cup dried Turkish apricots, pitted
1 cup dried prunes, pitted
1 cup raisins
3 cups apple juice
2 cups orange juice
1 cinnamon stick
12 oz. fresh cranberries

Place all the ingredients except for the cranberries in a medium pot. Cover and bring to a boil. Reduce heat to low and simmer for 30 minutes. Add cranberries – cover & simmer on a low heat for 10 minutes. Remove from heat and allow to cool at room temperature. Remove cinnamon stick.

Chill, except if serving as a dessert with ice cream, which is then best if served slightly warm spooned over the ice cream.

GLOSSARY

ANCHO PEPPER - a large, dried, mildly hot dark reddish brown poblano chili - used extensively in Mexican and Southwestern cooking.

ANCHOVY PASTE - smushed anchovies in a tube... very convenient when only a small amount of anchovy is needed.

ARAME SEAWEED - a dried delicate algae high in protein, potassium, calcium and other minerals. The light wiry threads have a sweet mild flavor... great added to soups, stir-frys and salads.

ARBORIO RICE - a white Italian rice with a creamy texture ⌐ primarily used for risottos.

BASMATI RICE - a fragrant white or brown Indian long-grained rice with a delicate nutty flavor.

BONITO FLAKES - the bonito fish is in the tuna family... the dried flakes are used in Japanese cooking to add flavor to stocks and dashi.

CHESAPEAKE BAY SEASONING - a combination

of ground herbs and spices used in seafood dishes - can be found in most markets.

CHILI OIL — a spicy vegetable oil steeped with hot red chili peppers ... widely used in Chinese cooking.

COCONUT MILK — widely used in Southeast Asian cooking, an unsweetened creamy thick milk made from coconuts ... can be found in ethnic sections of most markets or at Oriental markets.

FISH SAUCE - called "Nam Pla" in Thai, an intense salty brown liquid usually made from anchovies... a mainstay in Southeast Asian cooking. High in protein and Vitamin B.

GARAM MASALA - a blend of ground spices extensively used in Indian cooking. There are many variations of garam masala using different combinations of spices — look for at Indian markets.

GARLIC — not only do we love it passionately, but study has shown it to be remarkably good for you. It helps reduce blood pressure, lowers cholesterol and triglyceride levels, strengthens the immune system, and inhibits the formation of carcinogens and the spread of cancer. It is an excellent source of Vitamin C, iron and potassium. Basically, it is a godsend!

<u>GOMASIO</u> - a condiment made of sesame seeds and salt that have been ground together. Sesame seeds are high in calcium. Sprinkle on salads... veggies... grains... fish...

<u>HOISON (or HOISIN) SAUCE</u> - a reddish brown, sweet, spicy, thick sauce made from fermented soybeans, sugar, five-spice powder and garlic- widely used in Chinese cooking.

<u>JASMINE RICE</u> - a white long-grained aromatic rice used in Thai cooking.

<u>KALAMATA (or CALAMATA) OLIVE</u> - a very flavorful dark purple olive marinated in wine vinegar.

<u>KOMBU</u> - a dark green sea vegetable, usually cooked with broths or beans. It adds flavor

as well as vitamins and minerals. Available at natural food stores.

MIRIN - a sweet low-alcohol Japanese rice wine. Adds much flavor to marinades, sauces and dressings.

MISO - a thick salty paste made from fermented soybeans, sometimes with the addition of grains. It is high in protein and B vitamins, used to flavor soups, marinades, sauces and dressings, and can be found in natural food and Japanese markets.

NORI - dark sheets of dried pressed seaweed - high in Vitamin A and protein. Nori helps break down cholesterol and emulsifies fat - used to make sushi, but can be toasted and shredded to be added to soups, salads, veggies and grains.

NUTRITIONAL YEAST - rich in protein, Vitamin B, phosphorus and other minerals. Available in powder or flakes, it has a wonderful nutty, almost cheese-like flavor. Use as a breading - add to soups, sauces, etc.

PALM SUGAR (or jaggery) – a honey-like, very sweet sugar that comes from the sap of palmyra palms. Can be found in Southeast Asian markets.

PANCHPURAN – a combination of 5 seeds, frequently used in Indian cooking.

PASILLA PEPPER – a mild to moderately hot purple-black dried pepper, with a rich, smoky, almost fruity flavor.

PERNOD – a licorice-flavored liqueur – adds an interesting subtle accent when added to soups and sauces.

PICKLED GINGER – slices of ginger that have been pickled in brine. Traditionally served with sushi.

PORCINI MUSHROOMS – also known as cèpes in France. A large wild mushroom with a smoky, woodsy flavor, and meaty texture. Most often found dried.

PORTOBELLO MUSHROOMS – a rather large and dubious-looking mushroom; its earthy flavor and meaty texture make it ideal for grilling or adding to soups, stews and sauces.

RED CURRY PASTE - the most commonly used Thai curry paste; its fragrant hot, rich flavor comes from a blending of many ingredients ~ can be found at some markets in their ethnic section, or at Southeast Asian markets. Keeps well in an air-tight container in the fridge or freezer.

RICE VINEGAR - an aged delicate-flavored vine-gar, made from unrefined red wine or fermented rice. Can be found in Oriental markets and natural food stores.

SEITAN ~ a traditional Japanese food, sometimes referred to as wheat gluten. It has a meaty tex-ture and mild flavor. Made by rinsing and kneading wheat flour repeatedly until only the gluten remains. It makes a good substitute for meat in stews, soups, sauces, etc. Can be found in natural food stores and Oriental markets.

SHIITAKE MUSHROOMS - a delicious versatile mush-room originally imported from Korea and Japan, though it is now being cultivated in the U.S. Its full-bodied earthy flavor enhances many dishes — it is said to be quite nutritious, containing properties that help to restore the immune system. Can be found in most markets, as well as in Oriental stores.

SOBA — a Japanese-style pasta made from buckwheat flour or a combination of buckwheat and whole wheat flour. Very delicious and high in protein. Can be found in natural food & Oriental markets.

SUSHI RICE — a white Japanese rice used primarily for sushi ... sold in Oriental markets.

SZECHUAN CHILI PASTE — a spicy paste made from fermented beans, red chili peppers & garlic. Widely used in Chinese cooking.

TAHINI — a thick paste made from ground sesame seeds. It is high in calcium ... mainly used in Middle Eastern cooking ... sold at most markets and natural food stores.

<u>TAMARIND PASTE</u> - a thick paste with a sweet & sour flavor made from the fruit of the tamarind tree. An essential ingredient in Southeast Asian & Indian cooking ∽ available at their markets.

<u>THAI BASIL</u> - also called anise or licorice basil... used widely in Southeast Asian cooking... easy to grow (look for seeds in herb catalogs).

<u>THAI PEPPER</u> - dried red chilies and fresh bird chilies are the most commonly used peppers in Thai cooking ∽ both are extremely hot.

<u>TOFU</u> - also known as bean curd ∽ a traditional Oriental food made from the soy milk that is extracted from ground soybeans. It has a bland flavor that readily takes on the flavors of that with which it has been cooked. It is high in protein, calcium, iron, phosphorus, potassium, Vitamin B-choline & vitamin E. It is low in saturated fats & is entirely free of cholesterol. A good protein source for strict vegetarians.

<u>TOMATILLOS</u> - also referred to as Mexican green tomato or husk tomato. Resembles a small green

tomato but it has a papery husk covering. They have a tart flavor ~ can be found fresh or canned in most markets ~ they are high in vitamins A & C, and are the basis for the popular Mexican Salsa Verde.

TURBINADO SUGAR - a raw sugar that has been steam-cleaned. Its yellowish coarse crystals have a delicate flavor that works well as a substitute for white sugar.

UDON - a Japanese pasta with a flat wide shape similar to fettuccine. They are made from a combination of whole wheat and unbleached white flour... making them nutritious but not heavy.

UMEBOSHI - a Japanese pickled plum often used in macrobiotic cooking, for its flavor and medicinal qualities. It is said to help establish the intestinal flora needed for good digestion. Sold at natural food stores and Oriental markets, either as the whole pickled plum or as a paste.

Index